DAVID LEWIS is chairman of the David Lewis Consultancy, an international consumer research firm with clients including Disney, Coca-Cola, Amazon, IKEA, L'Oréal, Toyota, British Airways, British Telecom, ICL and IBM. He lectures in Europe, the USA and Asia on management topics, with a special emphasis on relationships between suppliers and their customers.

A bestselling author and broadcaster for both television and radio – his BBC radio series was the winner of the prestigious Sony Award – his recent books include *Information Overload*, *Ten-Minute Time and Stress Management*, and *How to Get Your Message Across*.

A Chartered Psychologist with a doctorate in Psychology from the University of Sussex, he is a fellow of both the International Stress Management Association and the Institute of Directors. He is also a member of the Marketing Society, the Market Research Society and the Institute of Direct Marketing.

DARREN BRIDGER is a researcher at the David Lewis Consultancy.

Praise for

The Soul of the New Consumer

"*The Soul of the New Consumer* is likely to shape the marketing messages you see, hear and read in the first years of the new century. The authors offer lucid analyses of a wide range of sales related issues, incorporating and building on the insights of a dazzling array of thinkers. For anyone in the business of sending those messages, it's an enlightening and compelling guide."
BookPage

"This is such an enjoyable book. And an important and timely one, too. David Lewis and Darren Bridger's book should become required reading."
Tim Waterstone, *Management Today*

THE SOUL OF THE NEW CONSUMER

THE SOUL OF THE
NEW CONSUMER

Authenticity –
What We Buy and Why
in the New Economy

Dr David Lewis
& Darren Bridger

NICHOLAS BREALEY
PUBLISHING

LONDON

In fondest memory of PEH

This updated paperback edition first published by
Nicholas Brealey Publishing in 2001

36 John Street
London
WC1N 2AT, UK
Tel: +44 (0)20 7430 0224
Fax: +44 (0)20 7404 8311

1163 E. Ogden Avenue, Suite 705-229
Naperville
IL 60563-8535, USA
Tel: (888) BREALEY
Fax: (630) 898 3595

http://www.nbrealey-books.com
http://www.NewConsumer.com

First published in hardback in 2000

Library of Congress Cataloging-in-Publication Data

Lewis, David, 1942-
    The soul of the new consumer : authenticity--what we buy and why in the new
economy / David Lewis & Darren Bridger.
        p. cm.
    First published in the U.K. in 1999.
    ISBN 1-85788-298-9 (pb.)
    1. Consumer behavior—History—20th century. I. Title: Authenticity – what we buy
and why in the new economy. II. Bridger, Darren. III. Title.

HF5415.32.L48 2001
658.8'342--dc21

00-054705

ISBN 1-85788-298-9

British Library Cataloguing in Publication Data
A catalogue record for this book is available from the British Library.

Printed in Finland by WS Bookwell.

Contents

Preface to the Paperback Edition

At the start of the twenty-first century we increasingly regard ourselves less as citizens of the world and more as customers in a global marketplace. In the industrialized nations, discussions of 'rights' are now more likely to reflect our role as consumers rather than our basic human or civil rights.

We are the New Consumers – independent minded, individualistic and well informed. We are cash rich and time poor. Bombarded by commercial messages, we remain deeply distrustful of hype and deeply disloyal to suppliers. We are the consumers on whose often spur-of-the-moment purchasing decisions depends the success or failure of businesses of all sizes.

What distinguishes New Consumers from those who came before us is not chronological age but attitudes toward consumption. Old Consumer attitudes were forged by the forces of mass production, mass marketing and mass consumption. Those of the New Consumers have been shaped by the seismic economic and social changes that began transforming industrialized societies from the late 1960s onward.

This rise in the influence and power of New Consumers has been mirrored by an exponential growth in the power and wealth of corporations. Of the world's top 100 economic entities, half are no longer countries but corporations. The merger of AOL and Time Warner in 2000, for example, created a corporation worth $350 billion. This is equal to the gross domestic product of India ($357.4 billion) and more than the combined GDPs of Hungary, Ukraine, the Czech Republic, New Zealand, Peru and Pakistan!

In part, the rise of both consumer and corporate power reflects the growing importance of information as the economic basis for growth and influence. Just as the printing press undermined the absolute authority of the church 500 years ago, the internet is threatening to undermine nation states and even the power of corporate giants whose policies are increasingly dictated by the power of market forces. After the break down of world climate talks at the Hague in November 2000, for example, George Kelly, director of the US industrial lobby group the Global Climate Coalition, admitted that the failure was less important than many observers believed, since: 'It is business, not government, that is developing new technologies. And business is being pushed by strong consumer demand, irrespective of governments or regulations.'[1]

As an example of the increasing voice that consumers will have in the marketplace, consider the Freenet software program (freenet.source-forge.net), which enables PCs on the net to swap files directly without the need for any intermediaries. Unlike Napster – the copyright-defying, song-swapping music exchange created in 1999 by 17-year-old Shawn Fanning – this software makes it impossible to discover who has posted or downloaded files, with the result that information can be exchanged between individuals with total anonymity. 'The implications,' suggests writer Mark Fischetti, 'are far-reaching. Whistle-blowers could post incriminating documents without fear of reprisals, and dissidents in totalitarian states could safely post anti-government rhetoric.'[2]

Over the years since my identification of – and with – New Consumers, I have been following their rise to economic prominence and observing their growing influence over the marketplace. My colleagues and I have explored their motives, and in over a thousand surveys examined their responses to everything from television commercials to the stress of shopping in malls and supermarkets.

We equipped our guinea-pig shoppers with miniature cameras to record their shopping experiences. We monitored such bodily responses as blood pressure and heart rate while they maneuvered laden trolleys along crowded supermarket aisles or stood in line to pay for purchases at busy checkouts. In our laboratory we analyzed electrical activity in the brain as they watched TV commercials and then related those responses to individual scenes in the advertisements.

In the chapters that follow I describe those research findings, explain the significance of our observations, and suggest the practical steps that manufacturers, suppliers and service providers must take in order to meet the challenges and seize the opportunities represented by the rise of the New Consumers.

Largely as a result of the growth of the internet, New Consumers are in a position to become better informed about companies, products and services than at any time in commercial history. They can investigate major corporations, gather lone voices of complaint or dissent into a genuine force for change, and compare prices, quality and delivery times around the world.

As well as wanting information, in an era of commodities New Consumers possess a strong desire for authenticity in many of the products and services they purchase. As I explain in Chapter 1, this quest for the authentic is partly driven by a need to express individuality through ownership of goods or services that are in some way innovative, original and different.

I examine not merely New Consumers' buying choices but their very soul. My use of the word 'soul' in this secular context may strike you as strange and inappropriate. Yet for many New Consumers the purchase of products and services has largely replaced religious faith as a source of inspiration and solace. For an even larger group, their buying decisions are driven by a deeply rooted psychological desire to develop and enhance their sense of self. Their choices are shaped by those core constructs from which identity and esteem are formed.

New Consumers are a group that you as a manufacturer, service provider or marketing specialist will remain ignorant of at your peril and ignore at your cost. They are the people on whom not merely your company's prosperity but its very survival will depend, for they possess the power to make or break any business, of any size, at any time.

As David Spangler, director of market research for the Levi brand, puts it: 'They are going to take over the country.'

Acknowledgments

Many books are, to varying degrees, collaborative efforts between the authors, their publishers and editors. This is very much the case with *The Soul of the New Consumer*, where the creative and practical input of our publisher Nick Brealey has played a significant role in shaping the final text. For this, as well as his support and encouragement, we are both extremely grateful.

We would also like to extend our sincere thanks to Sue Coll at Nicholas Brealey for her always constructive suggestions and to our tireless editor, Sally Lansdell, for her significant contribution to the form of the final manuscript.

We should also like to extend our thanks to ICL, and especially Yvette Asscher, Marketing Manager, Retail Systems Division, for taking the time to provide valuable insights into the future of retailing. Similarly, our thanks go to Professor Jon Bareham, Professor of Marketing at Brighton University, for offering such perceptive insights into trends in retailing. And to Dr Kathy Hammond, a consumer behavior expert, Director Future Media Research, at the London Business School, whose answers to many of our questions smoothed the early stages of research. Dr Doug Stewart, of the University of Greenwich, and Dr James Demetre, a developmental psychologist at the same university, were good enough to find time in their busy schedules to provide information, advice and guidance. Professor Burton Brodo, of Drexel University, Philadelphia, was kind enough to offer lengthy responses to our queries. Our thanks to Young & Rubican and Pirelli, and Royal Insurance for allowing us to use photographs taken from their television commercials.

We would also like to thank Mark Wentworth for his time, help and encouragement in researching the fascinating topic of cool hunters and to Cynthia Hemming, maven extraordinary and managing director of my consultancy, for her contribution to our knowledge and her enormous patience while the book was being written.

We are grateful to Julian Grainger of the National Film Institute and film director Tony Cornford for their input into the changing nature of television commercials.

Finally, a note of thanks to all the staff of the David Lewis Consultancy, especially IT manager James Breen, for their assistance in researching this book.

1

From Abundance to Authenticity: The Rise of the New Consumers

In the second half of the 20th century, we have gradually learnt to talk and think of each other and ourselves less as workers, citizens, parents or teachers and more as consumers.
Yiannis Gabriel and Tim Lang, The Unmanageable Consumer

American author and poet Shel Silverstein has coined the word Tesarac to describe those periods in history when momentous social and cultural changes occur. During a Tesarac, society becomes increasingly chaotic and confusing before reorganizing itself in ways that no one can accurately predict or easily anticipate. It is an era when, in the words of MIT's Shelley Turkle: 'Old things are dead or dying and one cannot easily make out what will happen next.'

Silverstein believes that the changes taking place as society travels through the Tesarac are so profound that nobody born one side of this 'wrinkle in time' will ever be able to understand fully what life was like before it occurred. A similar view has been expressed by Peter Drucker who, in his book *Post-Capitalist Society*, describes how, every few centuries, western society crosses what he terms a 'divide'. He cites the changes that took place in eighteenth-century Europe when the center of communal life moved from the countryside into the city. Craft guild members became the dominant social group, scholarship abandoned isolated monasteries for new universities at the heart of urban life, Latin gave way to the vernacular and Dante laid the foundation stones of European literature. 'Within a few short decades, society rearranges itself,' says Drucker, 'its world view; its basic values; its social and political structure, its arts; its key institutions. Fifty years later there is a New World. And the people born then cannot even imagine the world in which their grandparents lived and into which their own parents were born.'

We are still passing through the Tesarac and cannot accurately predict what the outcome will be. What is already apparent, however, is that manufacturers and suppliers trapped on the wrong side of this wrinkle in time will find themselves increasingly overwhelmed by the vastness of the changes it portends. Their more flexible, better-informed and astute competitors who have moved through the Tesarac and understand the nature of the New Economy will be able to tap into the change and sweep onward to undreamed-of levels of success.

Prior to the Tesarac, a significant driving force behind consumption was a desire to improve one's social class by acquiring material possessions, such as a new car, a television, freezer and furnishings, that would signify membership of the middle class. Today a majority of consumers have largely exhausted the things they *need* to purchase and are focusing instead on what they *want* to buy, that is, opportunities and experiences that claim to make their lives happier, richer and more rewarding. In the New Economy the companies most likely to succeed are those that enable New Consumers to make these investments of time, attention and money simpler to perform and more rewarding to experience.

In the world of the Old Consumer, every major aspect of a transaction, from the price paid and the distribution channels available, was dictated by manufacturers and suppliers. In the New Economy power is shifting more and more to consumers, who are increasingly able to dictate not only what they buy but how and where those purchases are

2

made – and even, with some products, what they are prepared to pay for them.

Take PriceLine.com, an internet company launched towards the end of 1998 with a market capitalization of $20 billion, whose purpose is to bring together buyers and sellers in an arena where the customer sets the pace. Rather than customers hunting for suppliers, manufacturers and service providers now come to PriceLine.com in order to find consumers. It is the customer who decides the price and the service providers or manufacturers who then accept or decline their business.

PriceLine's initial, well-publicised service focused on airline tickets, with potential travelers stating how much they are willing to pay for travel to any destination on a particular day and guaranteeing – by means of a credit card – that they will take the best seat available no matter what time the flight departs. Airlines with space on the route then bid for that passenger, solving their problem of filling empty seats on an almost minute-by-minute basis. Given that, on any day, there are some half a million empty seats in US airspace alone, even a low-paying passenger is preferable to a no-paying one.

From Scarcity to Abundance – from Abundance to Authenticity

The past few years have seen the rise and rapid growth in economic importance of a group of consumers whose attitudes, aspirations and purchasing patterns are unlike any before them. Already a potent force in the developed world, within the next decade they will come to dominate consumption in North America, Europe and Asia. On their decisions to buy or not to buy will depend not only your company's prosperity but also its very survival.

These are the New Consumers.

New, because their style of consumption is so distinctive, and Consumers, rather than customers, because these differences of approach influence every aspect of their purchasing decisions: from choosing which brand of baked beans to pluck from a supermarket shelf to whether to accept social changes, government policies, spiritual beliefs and political ideologies.

New Consumers transcend all ages, ethnic groups and even, to some extent, income. You are as likely to find them among the affluent over-fifties as in the ambitious under-thirties. When US record company Camelot analyzed its purchase data it discovered that the largest consumers of rap and techno music were not young people but grannies and granddads buying the music as presents for their grandchildren. After the company created a newsletter to keep this group in touch with the latest trends in pop music, its turnover rose by almost 40 percent.

Although when they first began to emerge in the marketplace New Consumers were predominantly male, the increasing economic power of women, both as wealth producers and consumer decision makers, means they are now equally likely to be of either sex.

Living in economies where their basic needs are quickly and easily satisfied, New Consumers are far more concerned with satisfying their wants, which frequently focus on original, innovative and distinctive products and services. As a result they tend to reject mass-produced and mass-marketed commodities in favor of products and services that can claim to be in some way authentic.

Independent, individualistic, involved and well-informed on consumer matters, they already rate as significant players in an increasingly fragmented and fragmenting marketplace. Every feature of the New Economy, from globalization to digitization, from new retailing technologies to internet shopping, has dramatically altered not only *how* New Consumers buy but *what* they buy and *why*.

No matter what product you manufacture or what service you sell, if you fail to understand not merely the behavior of these radically different consumers but their very soul, your once successful marketing strategies will crash headlong into their distrust and disinterest and your profits will plunge.

Manufacturers and service providers whose mindset still revolves around notions of mass production, mass marketing and mass consumption are already experiencing falling sales and eroding brand value. In 1999, for example, Levi's – which only two years earlier had been rated the world's eighth greatest brand – announced it was to close half its North American factories, following a 13 percent decline in sales.

Exactly why such events are happening and why many marketing specialists are becoming increasingly gloomy about the future of even well-established product-based brands will be discussed in detail later in this book. But the short answer is that global empires like Levi Strauss, Kelloggs, Woolworth, Marks & Spencer and even Coca-Cola – whose profits plummeted 27 percent in the fourth quarter of 1999 – have been paying insufficient attention to the attitudes and aspirations of these New Consumers.

The Anatomy of the Soul

The New Consumer that is emerging on the other side of the Tesarac is shown in Figure 1.

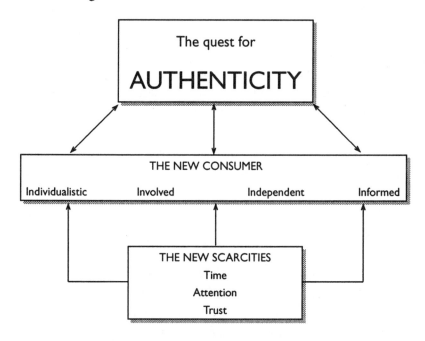

Figure 1 The soul of the New Consumer

The New Consumers were born into a society that was slowly moving away from years of austerity caused first by the great depression of the 1920s and early 1930s and subsequently by the Second World War. Postwar shortages and rationing placed great power in the hands of manufacturers and suppliers. For more than a decade after the war ended customers, rendered dutiful and conformist by years of restrictions, gratefully bought whatever producers deigned to sell them. Even as shortages eased, manufacturers continued to assume that mass production and mass marketing would allow them to continue regulating mass consumption. They were strongly supported in this view by advertisers, who saw their primary task as mass-producing consumers. In a presidential address to the American National Council on Family Relations in the late 1940s, for example, sociologist Clark Vincent explained that the family could now be regarded less as a 'production unit' and more as a 'viable consuming unit'.[1]

Where Old Consumers were beset by scarcities of cash, choice and availability, those confronting the New Consumer are shortages of time, attention and trust.

Whereas the Old Consumer was synchronized, usually uninvolved in production, conformist and often woefully uninformed, New Consumers are individualistic, involved, independent and generally well informed.

Perhaps the most significant change, and it is one that I shall discuss in detail in Chapter 2, is that while Old Consumers were largely motivated by a need for convenience, New Consumers are driven by a quest for authenticity.

Scarcities of time

New Consumers constantly grumble about there being too few hours in the day to satisfy all the demands made on them. Unfortunately, longer hours does not mean that all the work is getting done. A study by the American Management Association showed that almost half of all middle managers say they now have more work to do than time in which to do it. This could help explain why eight out of ten New Consumers fret about imbalances in their life, caused by having too

Because they are such individualists, no two New Consumers have exactly the same attitudes towards consumption, but the following two, whom I know well from my research, illustrate many of their key qualities.

Sam is a 27-year-old radio producer living with his girlfriend, Jo. They both work long and highly irregular hours, which means that free time is at a premium and 24-hour shops and the internet are shopping necessities.

'I tend to visit the big supermarkets because they have such a wide range of products,' says Sam, 'and the greatest benefit of shopping for groceries at two o'clock in the morning is that you never get caught in a queue. I hate doing the shopping when the aisles are packed and you have to hang around at checkouts. In fact, I often walk out and leave my trolley when the checkout lines are too long.'

For recreation Sam goes canoeing, making long expeditions on his own and enjoying the solitude of the river after working with people all week. 'It's my way of unwinding,' he explains.

Sam is attracted by anything new, cool and still unfashionable. Once everybody starts using or wearing a product, he tends to move on to something new. 'I keep myself informed about consumer issues and check the labels on unfamiliar products,' he comments. 'I like to make up my own mind about things and hate being told what to think.'

When tracking down furnishings and ornaments for their apartment, he and Jo visit street markets and secondhand shops, rather than high-street stores, in search of items that are in some way unique or original, although not necessarily expensive. 'I love old, authentic things in a modern flat,' he explains. 'It gives you a sense of balance and continuity.'

For Ann, a 36-year-old company director, look, style, subtlety and understatement are essential before she is attracted to any product: 'I buy designer-label clothes from Jil Sander, Max Mara and Nichole Fahri, but I don't want people necessarily to recognize the label,' she explains.

Ann keeps herself well informed via magazines such as Marie Claire and Good Housekeeping. She subscribes to these because she would rarely have to time to go out and buy them and also because this makes them cheaper. A self-confessed car freak, who drives a BMW 5 series, Ann also subscribes to motoring and computer magazines.

'I buy all my CDs off the internet, plus electronic equipment, partly because there is so much more choice and partly because it is cheaper to do so,' says Ann. 'I also buy organic vegetables, which are delivered once a week with the earth still on them.'

For recreation, Ann enjoys very early music as well as twentieth-century minimalist music by composers such as Steve Reich. 'There is a similarity to the structure of his work and, for example, Gregorian chants,' she says. 'I find repetition accompanied by slight change extremely de-stressing.'

An independent-minded shopper, Ann prefers to make her purchases on her own: 'I have no need for someone to approve or disapprove of what I buy,' she explains. 'I make up my mind very quickly, and never go from shop to shop comparing products. In most cases I know immediately whether or not a particular product is "me".'

Ann's passion is collecting silver, a hobby that she was quick to point out she started long before it became so fashionable. 'Silver is always utterly authentic without ever appearing flashy,' she explains.

little time to spend on their relationships, their family, hobbies and leisure activities. The results are rising stress levels and a desire to save time by almost any means, even if this involves paying for additional help or extra service. While such pressures affect Old and New Consumers alike, the latter are more likely to accept their fate while the former actively, although not always successfully, seek to reduce these burdens. Intolerant of delays and frequently cash rich, many New Consumers are prepared to pay a premium for the privilege of not being kept waiting. Organizations that can provide the almost instant gratification of needs twenty-four hours a day are set to gain a loyal following among a significant proportion of time-poor New Consumers.

One company that has grown huge by meeting this insatiable demand for having it 'now' is Viking Direct, the world's largest supplier of office stationery. Started in the 1980s, it now has over 2.5 million active business customers in 19 countries, from the US, the UK and Europe through to Australia, the Middle East, Africa and Asia. 'The overriding factor behind our success is our dedication to fanatical customer service,' says Brian Poll, the company's merchandising projects director.[2] Part of that 'fanatical service' is satisfying its customers' need for a by-return service. Orders placed one day will be delivered the next, while consumers living near a depot often get them the same day.

Another company cashing in on the time poverty of New Consumers is Screwdriver, set up in 1996 in the UK to help people who have bought flat-pack furniture from companies such as Ikea to put it together. Founder Jack Bock discovered that half of all furniture is sold as self-assembly and realized that there must be thousands of time-poor customers willing to pay extra to have their DIY purchases expertly assembled. He was right, and his company now has an annual turnover in excess of £1 million.

Scarcities of attention

Scarcities of time mean that New Consumers also frequently suffer from a scarcity of attention. Unless they are able to understand something quickly and easily it will often be ignored, especially when the personal relevance of the information is unclear. Partly as a result of time scarcity, younger New Consumers especially have developed greater visual literacy than any generation before them. They are able to understand and enjoy the complex, rapidly changing images found in computer games, pop music videos, many television commercials and films: sequences of fast-moving visual messages that would have baffled earlier generations of viewers. Indeed, the perceptual skills of these youngsters is often so advanced that they might be more appropriately called not teenagers but screenagers. They are also able to spot the strategies behind advertisements, with the result that conventional methods of persuasion often fail to move them.

Over the next ten years, companies will have to devise new and startling forms of advertising, based on images rather than words, in order to capture a little of the New Consumer's scarce attention, a point that I shall discuss in detail in Chapter 8. Already, for example, one advertiser is talking seriously about using lasers to project slogans on to the surface of the moon!

Scarcities of trust

While New Consumers are neither more nor less trusting than Old Consumers in their personal relationships, they are significantly less likely to offer unquestioning trust to suppliers. Research by the Henley Centre, for example, has shown that while nine out of ten people will trust their spouse or partner and eight out of ten their children, less than a third (27 percent) trust retailers or manufacturers, while just 14 percent trust either the government or advertisers!

Dissatisfaction is often a more likely outcome among those New Consumers whose lifestyles are characterized by high expectations and a desire for instant gratification. With high quality and value for money as 'givens', they are continually searching for products or services with the most value-added extras. Since loyalty takes time to build, the company that is first in the field often reaps the greatest rewards, provided that it maintains the highest levels of quality and service.

The quest for authenticity

At the heart of the soul of the New Consumer lies a desire for authenticity. 'People are called to authenticity, it is a vocation,' says journalist Bryan Appleyard. 'It has become the crucial moral orthodoxy of our time.'[3] In this quest they are prepared to put themselves to considerable inconvenience, sometimes traveling far from the beaten track to obtain whatever product it is they are eager to buy. Inventor James Dyson, for example, takes a great deal of trouble to purchase what he regards as the most authentic olive oil: 'I drive a long way to buy it from La Famille Chancel at Chateau Val Joannis, in Pertuis near Aix-en-Provence,' he says. 'It's full and aromatic; you can drink it like wine.'[4]

Both Nikon and Leica produce excellent, top-of-the-range cameras used by both professional and serious amateur photographers around the world. Yet while Nikons are generally regarded as a commodity, the Leica has achieved an aura of authenticity that allows it to appreciate in value over time. Oskar Barnack, a German engineer and mountaineering enthusiast who wanted an easily portable camera to accompany him on expeditions, designed the initial Leica shortly before the First World War. In the days of large-format photography, Barnack's groundbreaking idea was to create a camera that, instead of cumbersome single plates, used strips of 35mm film manufactured for the movie industry. By 1924, his friend Ernst Leitz had put this prototype into production and modern photography was born. Today the latest Leica, with a range of lenses, can cost in excess of $10,000 despite, or even because of, the fact that it lacks many of the high-tech features found on most modern Japanese cameras, such as auto focus and power winder.

When introduced in 1954 a M3 Leica sold for just a few hundred dollars. Today, in 'mint' condition, the same camera could fetch $5000 or more. Over the same period a Nikon F4, fine camera though it is, would become virtually worthless.

In part the perceived 'authenticity' of the Leica in relation to other models may lie in the fact that it has been used by such internationally celebrated photographers as Henri Cartier-Bresson and Lord Snowdon. Mainly, however, it resides in the camera's exceptionally high engineering and quality of construction. The Leica, as with all other exclusive and original products and services, possesses what the Japanese call *miryokuteki hinshitsu*, quality that fascinates, rather than simply *atarimae hinshitsu*, quality that is expected.

Atarimae hinshitsu represents the absolute minimum that New Consumers will accept – anything less and they feel cheated. But it is for *miryokuteki hinshitsu*, the quality that fascinates, that they have developed the most voracious appetite. It is a standard that manufacturers and service providers in the New Economy must increasingly strive to achieve in order to endow their brands with authenticity. For it is only by doing so that they can expect to capture the attention and win the trust of demanding New Consumers.

The rise of independent-minded New Consumers means that while the individual reigns supreme, society has been downgraded in importance. When the *Titanic* sank in the 1958 British film *A Night to Remember*, it was portrayed as a public disaster with important lessons for passenger safety. When the ship went down in James Cameron's 1997 production, it was presented in terms of a highly romantic personal tragedy. 'Between these two films,' says journalist Bryan Appleyard, 'the public realm vanished, to be replaced by the private realm of the authentic self and its fulfilment.'

With work, family and society no longer providing as ready a means of self-actualization as in the recent past, people are increasingly seeking authenticity in one of two ways: through spirituality and through 'retail therapy'.

Consuming spirituality

Spirituality has become an all-purpose description of what people feel to be missing from their lives rather than of what they hope to discover. According to Mick Brown, author of *The Spiritual Tourist*, this spiritual search is: 'A symptom of collective uncertainty in an age when the traditional institutions of church, family and community appear to be breaking down. A symptom too of growing disenchantment with the values of materialism, and a weariness of science, which has stripped all mystery out of existence.'

Because many New Consumers regard traditional religions as too dogmatic and even, in some cases, failing to offer an 'authentic' spiritual experience, there is an increasing interest in what many theologians regard as fringe or even pseudo faiths.

As Wade Clark Roof comments in *Spiritual Marketplace*:

There is considerable fluidity. There's a continuing hunger to find spiritual truth, but they have a clearer sense now that some of the things they looked to deliver them earlier, like consumption and materialism, don't work too well ... I see a more diverse, perhaps more individualistic religious and spiritual future.

Wealthy New Consumers are hiring a variety of spiritual advisers including personal yogis, meditation teachers, spiritual directors and smudgists – Manhattanite home cleaners who turn up complete with rattles, drums and incense to spiritually purify the home. Stores selling a vast range of New Age products, candles, incense, crystals, essential oils, rock formations, magnets, as well as books on every aspect of the spiritual quest are spreading rapidly through towns and cities on both sides of the Atlantic. Many of these books, tapes and videos offer alienated New Consumers the promise of feeling more relaxed, more peaceful and more fulfilled, of discovering harmony, inspiration, energy and enlightenment.

The sales of more mainstream religious books increased by 150 percent between 1991 and 1997, in sharp contrast to the 35 percent rise for secular books. Even non-religious guides to everyday contentment became more popular, like *Simple Abundance* and *Don't Sweat the Small Stuff*. The latter is one of the Chicken Soup series, the most successful in publishing history, with over 30 million copies currently in print.

As Alvin Toffler puts it: 'Today we see millions desperately searching for their own shadows, devouring movies, plays, novels, and self-help books, no matter how obscure, that promise to help them locate their missing identities.'

Consuming produce

We live in a society where common ideals and political resolve have been largely replaced by shared meanings revolving around brand names and advertising images. As sociologist John Clammer observes: 'Shopping is not merely the acquisition of things, it is the buying of identity.'

Wealthy Old Consumers frequently go in for conspicuous consumption, flaunting gold Rolexes, Mercedes sports coupés, designer suits, marble bathrooms with gold taps and champagne always on ice. They display these and similar high-price trophies in much the same way as an earlier generation of big game hunters would garnish their library walls with the heads of their prey.

Many well-heeled New Consumers, by contrast, are eschewing blatant displays of wealth in favor of more subtle demonstrations of financial muscle. Gold Rolexes, for example, can be bought at the counter of almost any high-class jewelers, but if you want the far less ostentatious steel one, you'll have to join a five-year waiting list. In downtown

Manhattan and Washington DC, mountain bikes with chunky tires and titanium frames are becoming more commonplace than flashy sports cars. Bespoke suits at business meetings are giving way to Gap khakis. In the bathrooms of stylish American homes, the trend is for stainless-steel regulation prison toilets, while refrigerators are more likely to stock beer than champagne.

These purchases don't represent the impact of any financial constraints, but rather the quest for authenticity. Indeed, the price tag on a minimalist lifestyle can run far higher than for an ostentatious one. Those sleek mountain bikes cost thousands of dollars, a regulation prison lavatory is ten times the price of a standard model, and the beers in the freezer are likely to have been micro brewed and cost as much as champagne cocktails. As a designer in a cartoon in *The New Yorker* put it while talking to a prospective client: 'Minimalist? I'm not sure if your budget is big enough for minimalism.'

Old Consumer-style conspicuous consumption typically involves the purchase of inauthentic products that, by their nature, can have no underlying sense of unity. New Consumers, through their emphasis on authenticity, ensure that even when their purchases are totally different, they still possess unity in terms of their originality and uniqueness.

New Consumers are individualistic

In 1952 an American psychologist named Solomon Asch asked university students to compare two lines and say whether one was longer, shorter or the same length as the other.[5] Students were tested in groups but only one was a genuine subject, the rest were his accomplices who had been instructed to give an identical wrong answer on certain trials. Asch's purpose was to discover whether the naïve individual would stick with his own – correct – answer or change his mind to conform to a majority opinion. The results were startling. Despite obvious differences between the two lines, when six other group members insisted that both were of the same length, 95 percent of the naïve subjects went along with the majority view. They voted for conformity against the clear evidence of their own eyes. When an attempt was made to repeat the experiment 30 years later, however, young people refused to be swayed by the opinions of their peers, insisting that, even if theirs was a lone voice, it was a truthful one.

The quest for authenticity obliges New Consumers to swim alone or in small groups rather than moving with the synchronized shoals of Old Consumers. They must leave themselves free to seek out the often subtle differences that distinguish the authentic product from the mass-produced commodity. In the words of Yiannis Gabriel and Tim Lang, New Consumers are continually engaged in a discourse of difference, an exploration of 'minute variations, of idiosyncrasies of style, products, brand, signs and meanings ... the discovery of difference, the establishing of difference and the appropriation of difference'. Freud used the phrase the 'narcissism of small differences' to describe the discrete ways in which we seek simultaneously to demonstrate our individuality and a membership of some small but select group.

On the sleeve of a suit by top British designer Paul Smith, for example, you will always find five or six buttons rather than the usual four. A BMW M5 is one of the fastest and most sought-after sports cars on the road, yet its only distinguishing feature from a similar car of the same make is a tiny M5 badge on the rear. A mere glance at a shirt collar is sufficient to tell a connoisseur whether it is hand made or mass produced. 'The collar of a good shirt has a certain softness and fluidity about it,' says clothing company founder Jeremy Hackett. 'The stitching should always be about a quarter of an inch from the edge. Too close or too far and you can tell it hasn't been properly done.'[6]

To the uninitiated such fine distinctions might pass unnoticed and unremarked. For New Consumers the differences are a matter of pride and reassurance. Not only do they indicate membership of an exclusive club, but they also carry the stamp of authenticity.

The desire for individuality is, then, both the means to an end – the confirmation of authenticity – and an end in itself, a subtle demonstration of personal uniqueness.

'The mythological homogeneous America is gone', says Joel Weiner, senior vice-president marketing for Kraft Foods. 'We are a mosaic of minorities.'

New Consumers are involved

To ensure authenticity, New Consumers must often involve themselves far more closely with the processes of production and/or consumption to ensure that what they buy exactly matches their needs. Ikea, for example, is popular among New Consumers who love its interactive appeal, the fact that they can bounce on the beds and handle the products, that the catalogs are informative and pass on valuable inside information, such as 'this chair looks great, but for something really comfortable to watch TV and eat dinner on there's a cheaper one that might suit you better'.

For many New Consumers, getting involved transforms even routine grocery shopping into a quest for products whose authenticity is seen as a way of safeguarding the family's health or satisfying their ethical principles:

◆ Are those eggs truly free range?
◆ Are those vegetables really organic?
◆ Does that processed food contain GM products?
◆ Were those clothes stitched by child labor?
◆ Was that shampoo tested on animals?

Old Consumers, although they sometimes involve themselves in creation or consumption, are generally more detached and accepting. They trust manufacturers and suppliers to provide them with goods and services that will live up to their expectations, without going into the matter in any great depth.

Many retailers are prospering by providing New Consumers with a chance to become involved with the products they are buying. One of the most unorthodox, some would even say eccentric, approaches comes from Lush, a company formed just over five years ago to sell fresh and handmade cosmetics.

Although its products are destined for the bathroom rather than the kitchen, Lush stores are fitted out in Provençal-style butcher's block wood, giving them the look and feel of a delicatessen or cheese shop.

Lush's founder, Mark Constantine, started making herbal hair and beauty treatments in 1974, selling his products through healthfood stores. His first big breakthrough came in a creative partnership with Body Shop founder Anita Roddick and for more than 15 years he was that company's main supplier.

One of the keys to Lush's worldwide popularity – in addition to 20 shops in the UK it has stores in Australia, Brazil, Canada, Croatia, Japan, Sweden and Singapore – has been to allow consumers to become involved in the retail process. Even its name came out of a competition among customers.

Customers are encouraged to interact with the products, to smell and touch them as they serve themselves from refrigerated cabinets or experiment with the ultimate in pick 'n' mix skincare at the cleansing bar. Shampoo bars and bath ballistics are piled into tiered wooden display stands and dusting powders are decanted from colored glass tanks into shaker tubs. Herbal hair colorants and treatments are sold warm from bain maries (steamers) and essential information about products and ingredients is spelt out on strategically positioned blackboards. Ingredients are also described by quantity on every label, a policy that Lush has followed since the launch of its retail stores in 1995.

Lush stores involve consumers in other ways as well, bombarding your senses with the compelling aroma of herbs, fruits, flowers, oils and essences the moment you set foot through the door. The counters are piled high with soaps, displayed whole in huge cakes and wrapped in sheets of white paper, looking exactly like loaves of freshly baked bread. Many cosmetics are sold by weight or size after being cut from blocks and offered with a minimum of packing or no wrapping at all.

Recognizing the ecological concerns of New Consumers, concerns that Mark Constantine shares, Lush guarantees that none of its products have been tested on animals.

With an annual turnover in excess of $30 million and still growing rapidly, Lush offers the perfect illustration of a niche retailer well in tune with New Consumer aspirations and attitudes.

New Consumers are independent

Convenience shopping, by its very nature, implies a conformist approach to consumption, since it is only by means of mass production and mass marketing that goods can be made widely available at competitive prices. New Consumers prefer to make up their own minds about purchasing decisions rather than being told what to buy. Anything that smacks of the hard sell, dogmatic assertion or glib sales talk is likely to arouse their suspicions and be denied their trust.

New Consumers assert their independence by challenging established thought and demanding that monologue is replaced by dialogue. Tolerant of ambiguity, they mistrust black-and-white messages, continually searching for meaning in the shades of grey between extremes.

Since New Consumers insist on making their own decisions about almost everything, from how to find spiritual fulfilment to where and when they go shopping, the most successful companies will be those that go out to them, instead of passively waiting for them to turn up on their doorstep. Given the fact that many New Consumers are, as already mentioned, time poor, this will inevitably lead to more and more products and services becoming available around the clock and virtually instantaneously.

New Consumers are well informed

Information is the fuel that drives the New Consumer. The internet has made it cheaper and more readily available than ever before. The attraction of information, at least in part, lies in the fact that it permits them greater control over their spending. It opens up avenues of choice and allows for more carefully reasoned judgments to be made about prospective purchases.

New Consumers check labels, study contents, compare prices, scrutinize promises, weigh options, ask pertinent questions and know their legal rights. 'The number of people reading labels is going up every year,' says American retail specialist Paco Underhill. 'We're reading nutritional labels. We're looking at that label and figuring something out. In short, we are becoming better, more active, consumers.'

New Consumers vs Old Consumers

These, then, are the New Consumers, the people to whom you will increasingly be selling your goods and services in the near future and among whom you may well count yourself. The table below summarizes the key differences between New and Old Consumers.

Old Consumers	New Consumers
Seek convenience	Seek authenticity
Synchronized	Individual
Less often involved	Involved
Conformist	Independent
Less well informed	Well informed

In describing the buying patterns of Old Consumers as synchronized, I mean that they are more likely to follow than to lead, to be late adopters of innovative products and services, and to feel more comfortable and secure when buying from the marketing mainstream than if branching out on their own.

These defining characteristics should be viewed not as rigid categories but rather as the opposite ends of a continuum:

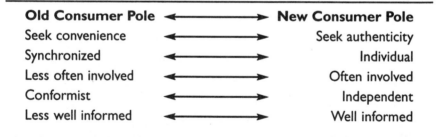

Old Consumer Pole		New Consumer Pole
Seek convenience	⟷	Seek authenticity
Synchronized	⟷	Individual
Less often involved	⟷	Often involved
Conformist	⟷	Independent
Less well informed	⟷	Well informed

While a minority of consumers may spend most of their time at one or other end of this continuum, the majority are capable of migrating, to various degrees, towards either pole according to circumstances.

Old Consumers, for example, may favor authenticity over convenience for certain purchases, just as New Consumers will sometimes opt for convenience over authenticity. Similarly, while a desire to become involved with the process of manufacturing or consuming occurs more frequently among New Consumers, it is not entirely absent from the Old. Finally, although mass-produced and mass-marketed products hold greater attraction to Old than New Consumers, the latter certainly devote much of their time to buying them, especially when this saves time.

What differentiates New from Old Consumers, therefore, is not their total acceptance or complete rejection of either pole on the continuum, but their preference for one end or the other and the characteristics of products or services that they are most likely to value most highly.

New Consumers 'R' Us

The fact that you have been interested enough to read this book suggests that you are among those who not only appreciate what serving the New Consumer will involve, but also find the prospect thrilling if somewhat daunting.

It is thrilling because of the vast opportunities it offers and daunting because you know the extent of the challenge that these New Consumers will pose to your managerial skills, your powers of innovation and imagination, as well as your courage in seizing those opportunities.

As I explained in the Foreword, my co-author and I regard ourselves as New Consumers – having read a little about their lifestyles, attitudes and aspirations you may well do the same.

But whether or not you recognize yourself in them, it is essential that you recognize their significance to your business. The New Consumers have arrived and nothing will ever be quite the same again. Within the next few years they are set to become the dominant economic social and political force in the marketplaces of the developed world.

Their decisions whether to buy or not to buy will be capable of making or breaking any company of any size at any time. Conscious that their time and attention are all too scarce, they will want advertisers to ask permission before approaching them and will expect to be rewarded for condescending to take notice. High-pressure, high-cost advertising hype will prove increasingly ineffective compared to powerful grassroots buzz, a topic we shall examine in depth in Chapter 5.

Mass-marketed commodities will fall by the wayside to be replaced by limited runs – in some cases limited to one – of products that are highly innovative, original and in some way stamped with the mark of authenticity.

Today, with high quality and low prices taken as givens by demanding New Consumers, the challenge facing companies is perfectly summarized by Gary Hamel and Jeff Sampler:

No more holding people hostage through 30-second commercials. No more hype. No more ignorant customers. No more local monopolies. No more search costs. No more 'Get in your car and come to us'. If you're paying attention, you're sweating by now.[7]

Summary

◆ The past four decades have seen the evolution of a new group of consumers, whose financial power and influence are now set to dominate the markets of the developed world.

◆ This tidal wave of change that originated in altered social and economic conditions following the Second World War has been accelerated in recent years by the arrival of e-commerce, the growth of the internet and the development of the New Economy.

◆ While Old Consumers often bought out of habit and were strongly influenced by the convenience of mass marketing and mass consumption, New Consumers adopt a more individual, involved, independent and informed approach to consumption.

◆ While the buying habits of Old Consumers were often dominated by product scarcities, New Consumers suffer scarcities of time and attention. As a result, they are often willing to pay premium prices in order to save both.

◆ Companies and individuals who understand and can meet these needs are those most likely to prosper in the New Economy.

◆ One of the most significant differences between Old and New Consumers is the latter's desire for authenticity. Exactly what this means in practice and ways in which companies may use this quest to their advantage will be explained in Chapter 2.

2

Persuading New Consumers: The Quest for Authenticity

The companies that are lasting are those that are authentic. If people believe they share values with a company, they will stay loyal to a brand.
Howard Schultz, Starbucks

In 1984 a former plastics salesman named Howard Schultz visited Italy and conceived of a great idea: 'It was like an epiphany,' he recalls. 'It was so immediate and physical that I was shaking.'

Milan, a city the size of Philadelphia, had 1500 expresso bars and in the country as a whole there were some 200,000. But what especially fascinated and impressed Howard Schultz was the deft manner in which the bartenders (*barista*) in these coffee houses created a demitasse of expresso or the foaming head on a cappuccino:

> *The barista moved so gracefully that it looked as though he were grinding the coffee beans, pulling shots of expresso, and steaming milk at the same time while conversing merrily with his customers. It was great theater.*[1]

Flying home, Schultz dreamed of a chain of US espresso bars that would recreate Milan's coffee-house culture. To ensure that Starbucks had an authentic feel from the start, Schultz spotlighted his *baristas* as though they were on a stage, ensured they were experts at their job and invented exotic, Italian-sounding names for his various drinks – for example a double espresso with a splash of milk was a *doppio macchiato*.

Today, Starbucks' profits are five times greater than the industry average. The company tells us a great deal about what it takes to develop a marketing concept that will appeal to the soul of the New Consumer. Although selling what used to be essentially a mass-produced and mass-marketed commodity, it artfully recreates the authentic look and feel and smell of genuine Italian coffee houses. The décor, which differs slightly from one shop to the next, is in earthy shades of brown and orange, with small tables and wicker baskets filled with newspapers. Thanks to its atmosphere of relaxed self-indulgence, Starbucks has become a safe 'third place' (see Chapter 6), a secure and friendly yet easily accessible public area where New Consumers can unwind, meet friends, enjoy agreeable conversations or sit alone savoring the aroma and reading a daily paper.

Starbucks' success has been good not only for Howard Schultz but for overall coffee sales, because the sense of authenticity it conferred on the brand extended even to jars on supermarket shelves. At the start of the 1990s only 3 percent of coffee sold in the US was priced at a premium, that is at least 25 percent higher than value brands. After Starbucks, the proportion is around 40 percent.

As Vijay Vishwanath and David Harding point out:

> *When individual companies increase the perceived 'premiumness' of a product through innovations in the product itself or the way it is delivered, the entire category can reap higher prices and rewards.*[2]

As I explained in the previous chapter, it is in their quest for authenticity that New Consumers differ most strikingly from the Old. But what exactly does the term mean?

Do you consider salmon reared in fish-farm pens to be as authentic as those that are caught in the wild? If you do, does your opinion change on being told that since the diets of farmed salmon are lacking in the nutrients necessary to give their flesh its distinctive rosy pink color, they must be fed chemicals, such as canthaxanthin, to restore their 'natural' (i.e. authentic) appearance?

The *Oxford English Dictionary* defines authenticity as 'genuine, reliable, trustworthy, real, actual, original and of established credit,' but as I shall demonstrate, the authenticity or otherwise of a product or service may in fact exist only in the eyes of the beholder.

Blurring the boundaries

The key to the massive commercial success of the 1999 film *The Blair Witch Project* is that it deliberately set out to deceive – or at least confuse – audiences as to its authenticity.

'We wondered what might happen if you could make a film where the audience members had no idea whether it was real or not, even after they left the theater – where there's nothing inherent in the film that tells you it's a lie,' said Eduardo Sanchez, the film's co-writer and director.

The Blair Witch Project was shot in Maryland using relatively unknown actors. For a further touch of authenticity, their real names were used for the characters they played. The cast, two men and a woman, were dumped in the woods, left to fend for themselves, and deliberately scared out of their wits by the filmmakers, sometimes using techniques adapted from those used by the US army.

Reputedly made for $22,000, the Hollywood equivalent of petty cash, the film has grossed more than $150 million at the box office, making it arguably the most commercially successful film in motion picture history, a success in a large part due to a deliberate blurring of the boundaries between realism and fakery.

'The acting is real, the lighting is real, the camera work is real, the quality of the videotape is real,' says Sanchez. 'The fact that our film is all handheld shots, like a home movie, allows you to get carried away more easily and it really fools people.'

No less intriguing that the movie's construction of 'authenticity' was the way in which interest in the completed movie was generated, especially among highly influential young American New Consumers, by low-cost buzz rather than high-priced hype. This is a topic to which I shall return in Chapter 5. The construction and subsequent commoditization of authenticity can be applied to a wide range of products and services, as the following examples show.

Creating an authentic ale

Before the 1970s there were no strong national UK beer brands; each region produced its own local brew whose popularity was as much a family matter as a regional one. Yorkshire males supped Yorkshire ales, because that was what their fathers and grandfathers had drunk before them. These ales were, therefore, regarded as authentic regional products and a matter of local pride.

The beer-drinking scene changed dramatically with the arrival of bigger brands in the late 1970s and early 1980s. The authenticity of these newcomers was sold on one of two premises: either that they came from countries renowned for their brewing such as Germany and Denmark, or that they were from places such as the US (Budweiser), Ireland (Guinness) and Australia (Fosters), whose inhabitants are recognized as world-class beer drinkers.

Thanks to their clear location in place (one of the routes to authenticity described later in this chapter), these beers were viewed by a majority of drinkers as authentic. They helped transform beer from a somewhat dull and untrendy drink into a young, cool and happening beverage. These new beers rapidly became the choice of New Consumers wanting to break with tradition and express their individuality and independence. In the third stage of development, brewers introduced packaged premium lagers. Some, such as Sol and Grolsch, were helped to stand out from the crowd by being packaged in original and innovative ways (yet another route to authenticity). Others, Becks for instance, used bottle designs which, in the words of John Grant, 'reinforced their "jeans like" earthy authenticity'.[3]

By the 1990s the wheel was turning full circle, with a consumer backlash against designer beers, and regional brands, such as John Smiths, Tetley's and Boddingtons (the Cream of Manchester), being marketed nationally. These achieved authenticity through their traditional image that restated the essential masculinity of beer as the drink of choice for an increasingly assertive and 'laddish' youth culture.

At the time of writing, the quest for authenticity by New Consumer beer drinkers has seen them embrace handmade ales from microbreweries and ice beers, as well as those from countries such as Japan, not previously seen as great beer producers. In the near future, however, I expect to see an increasing interest in creating authentic brews at home as technology makes the process sufficiently rapid and uncomplicated to appeal to time-scarce New Consumers.

Tom Keating's authentic fakes

In 1976 a scandal erupted in the art world after it was discovered that a painting by the nineteenth-century English landscape artist Samuel Palmer, just sold at auction for some £10,000, was a fake.

Tom Keating, a well-known picture restorer, quickly confessed to faking that picture as well as eight others bearing Palmer's signature. He estimated that there were around 2500 of his forgeries, or Sexton Blakes (Cockney rhyming slang for fakes), in galleries and private art collections around the world. He was arrested and sent for trial, but all charges were later dropped due to his poor health.

The most intriguing aspect of this story is not that a great many eminent critics and collectors were taken in by Keating's Sexton Blakes, but that his pictures soon became valuable and eagerly sought after – not as authentic works by famous painters, but as authentic fakes by a famous forger.

If you can have genuine fakes, can you also transform kitsch into authentic art merely by changing the way it is made?

Fake flowers – authentic art or artful kitsch?

A few years ago while lecturing on authenticity in Florida, I asked members of my audience to name products they found inauthentic. One of them, a wealthy widow in her sixties, mentioned her deep loathing of artificial flowers, which she considered a supreme example of all that is inauthentic.

Accepting an invitation to visit her lavish ocean-front apartment, I was astonished to find bouquets of artificial blooms decorating every room. When I challenged her on this apparent contradiction, she replied in affronted tones that by 'inauthentic' she had meant the crudely mass-produced sort that one found in discount stores. Her blossoms, she told me indignantly, were works of art, each one hand crafted in wax and costing a small fortune.

The marketing potential of pseudo authenticity in the New Economy is well illustrated by plans to construct an exact, $600 million replica of the *Titanic*.[4]

Two companies, one South African and the other Swiss, are currently in the advanced stages of plans to build a vessel that follows the original designs as accurately as possible, even to the extent of providing steam engines coupled to modern diesels. One of the main reasons that more than 1500 lives were lost in 1912 was that the original vessel was equipped with insufficient lifeboats; in order to maintain the accuracy of the replica's appearance many of the lifeboats are to be concealed behind metal screens. To add even greater authenticity to the project, the Basle-based company has bought the name of the White Star Line, owners of the ill-fated original, and the South African RMS Titanic Shipping Holdings has been in contact with Harland & Wolff, the Belfast shipyard that built the first one.

Not only do the backers expect the vessel to be a sellout for passengers, but they estimate that a further $100 million can be earned through merchandising everything from T-shirts to caps.

The Lure of Authenticity

Why it is that New Consumers are so eager to possess and experience the authentic, even when that authenticity has been painstakingly manufactured and is entirely ersatz?

The most obvious answer is that 'authentic' products and services offer the best value for money since they are superior in quality, more reliable in use and likely over time to maintain their value, or even increase it. While this is often all true, it is not the only or in many instances even the most important consideration. Many products that New Consumers reject as inauthentic offer just as much quality, reliability and value for money as those perceived to possess an aura of authenticity.

In addition, the variations in design and manufacture that distinguish the two are frequently so slight and subtle – remember Freud's 'narcissism of small differences' to which I referred in Chapter 1 – that only an expert would notice any difference. Underlying the lure of authenticity, therefore, is something far more central to the soul of the New Consumers: self-fulfilment. In their quest for the authentic, New Consumers are really seeking to discover themselves. Not the people they feel themselves to be at this moment, but the kind of men and women they aspire to be and feel it is within their power to become.

Authenticity, Alienation and Self-Actualization

As the West began moving through the Tesarac, social rules and conventions that for decades had helped people establish and maintain their sense of identity started to break down and a gap began to appear between two key aspects of self-image. On one side of this divide is our real self, the person we perceive ourselves to be, and on the other our ideal self, the person we are striving to become. This ideal self serves as a beacon guiding us towards our goals in life. In the words of Harvard psychologist Gordon Allport:

Every mature personality may be said to travel towards a port of destination, selected in advance, or to several ports in succession, their Ideal Self always serving to hold the course in view.[5]

American psychologist Abraham Maslow, a founder of the humanist school of psychology, describes this continual striving to become our ideal self as self-actualization. Maslow argued that to achieve self-actualization one must move up the pyramid of human needs – for example, one can hardly be expected to appreciate beauty if every waking moment involves a desperate struggle to satisfy hunger and thirst. Similarly, even paying attention to an informative book becomes difficult is one if too cold, too hot or in physical danger. Since each one of us must follow our own path to personal fulfilment, the further up the hierarchy we progress the more closely needs become linked to our life-experiences:

Self-actualization is idiosyncratic, since every person is different ...The individual (must do) what he, individually, is fitted for. What a man can be, he must be.[6]

As abundance in the developed world reduces the need to struggle for basic necessities, New Consumers are freed to devote more time, effort and energy to closing the gap between their real and ideal selves. Their quest for authenticity stems from this relentless striving for self-actualization.

Unfortunately, the harder we strive to attain our ideal self the further away it seems to be, and the wider the gulf that exists between it and our real self. This leads of feelings of alienation as we increasingly find ourselves separated not only from our ideal self but even from those closest to us. Father Joseph Keegan claims that outside of themselves modern man (or woman) has:

no compelling cause, no issue, no group with which he can truly identify. Thus lost and stranded, his basic identity has either vanished or become so nebulous as to be practically non-existent.

While I regard this view as overly pessimistic, it is apparent that a degree of alienation permeates the lives of even the most apparently successful and ambitious people. As MIT historian Bruce Mazlish comments:

> *Whereas ... the nineteenth century was marked by the classical neuroses of hysteria and obsession, the twentieth century is characterized by narcissistic disorders, the 'empty self'.*[7]

Such an identity crisis inevitably occurs in any society passing through a Tesarac. As social roles become less clearly defined, the rules and conventions by which individuals previously regulated their lives no longer apply. Zygmunt Bauman, author of *Intimations of Post Modernity*, considers that in western societies at least the work ethic has been replaced by the consumer ethic:

> *The same central role which was played by work, by job, occupation, profession in modern society, is now performed in contemporary society by consumer choice. The former was the lynch-pin which connected life-experience – the self-identity problem, life-work, life-business – on the one level; social integration on the second level; and systematic production on the third level.*

Other writers such as David Corten have suggested that our pursuit of material wealth and possessions reflects an attempt to fill a void left in our lives by a lack of love:

> *It is a consequence of dysfunctional societies in which money has displaced our sense of spiritual connection as the foundation of our cultural values and relationships.*[8]

Corten sees this relentless struggle for money as creating an ever-widening gap between individuals, their families and their communities. The result is deepening alienation, leading to an inner sense of social and spiritual emptiness.

Liking and authenticity

In an eighteenth-century essay by the French writer Denis Diderot, he describes his joy on being given a wonderful new dressing gown. Unfortunately, set against this magnificent garment his other possessions appeared so shabby that he set about replacing first one, then another. Before long Diderot's dissatisfaction was so great that he had replaced everything he owned, including furnishings, pictures, ornaments, clothes and even shoes. When the transformation was complete, Diderot could only reflect nostalgically on how much happier and more comfortable he had been in his former humble, crowded and chaotic workroom. 'Now the harmony is destroyed,' he wrote sadly. 'Now there is no more consistency, no more unity, and no more beauty.'

Diderot's lament illustrates the fact that consumption does not involve a series of unrelated purchases, but a need to achieve consistency between and within an ever-growing variety of possessions.

Grant McCracken describes the objects with which we surround ourselves as both 'bulletin boards for internal messages and billboards for external ones'. These messages, he believes, are communicated not by any one thing, but by all the objects working in concert, an effect he terms Diderot unity. Once this unity disappears, after a single element in our surroundings changes, the harmony is disrupted and further changes become inevitable. 'According to this view,' say Yiannis Gabriel and Tim Lang, 'individual purchases are not motivated by envy or social competition or display, but by an urge for consistency and completeness.' People are also motivated to purchase or experience products and services that they like and perceive as authentic.

In one of a number of experiments that I conducted in order to explore the relationship between liking and authenticity, I asked New Consumers to rate their liking for a small green glass bottle on a scale of 1 (not at all) to 5 (a great deal). Some were told nothing about the history of this bottle, while others were informed that it had been discovered in the ruins of Pompeii, the ancient city of Campania buried by the eruption of Mount Vesuvius in AD79. Those who believed they were holding an authentic relic from the catastrophe rated their liking between 4 and 5, with several going into raptures over the beauty of the patina, the elegance of the design and the luster of the color. When asked how much they would pay to possess it, many made offers running into hundreds of dollars.

None of those given the bottle without any information as to its origins expressed any particular liking for it (ratings 1–2), considered it especially attractive or expressed any interest in owning it. From this is seems clear that, as a general rule, if we perceive something to be authentic we are more likely to like it.

In the next part of the experiment I tested the extent to which the liking for a product can make it appear more authentic, by asking the same New Consumers to similarly rate their liking for a small, barnacle-encrusted figurine. They were then told that it was believed to have come from the *Titanic* and asked to rate the extent to which they considered this true. Those who liked the object most were more inclined to believe it had come from the *Titanic* than those who disliked it. However, among the people who neither liked nor disliked it to any great extent (rating 3), those who believed the story was true increased their liking for it, while those who dismissed the tale as a fabrication disliked it even more.

The same experiment conducted among Old Consumers showed them to be far less affected by the provenance. Those given the supposed age and origins of the bottle considered the information 'interesting' without its increasing their liking for the item. Similarly, irrespective of the extent to which they liked or disliked the statue, they were far more willing to take the story of it having come from the *Titanic* at face value. In other words, any 'authenticity' bestowed on the item by its supposed origin made much less impact on Old than on New Consumers.

This finding that liking for a product or service encourages New Consumers to regard it as authentic holds just as true for brands, with those considered to offer a highly authentic product or experience, such as Disney, Apple, Virgin Atlantic, Starbucks and The Body Shop, also being among some of the best-liked companies.

The association between brand identity and consumer liking was demonstrated in an intriguing study by Mark DiMassimo of the New

York-based DiMassimo Brand Advertising agency.[9] In 1999, when Clinton was deeply mired in the impeachment crisis, DiMassimo analyzed the feelings of different brand users towards the President.

He discovered that 84 percent of regular Campbell soups consumers supported Clinton's dismissal from office, the highest such figure for any brand covered in the study. Also strongly supporting impeachment were consumers loyal to Oscar Mayer hot dogs (79 percent), Fantastik cleaner (76 percent) and Tide detergent (75 percent). DiMassimo commented that all these anti-Clinton brands enjoy long-running traditions of consumer trust:

> *These are the old standbys. Who knows why people like Tide? It's just a brand, a purely iconic sort of thing. So people who are loyal to these sort of brands are into loyalty in general.*

They would therefore tend to be less tolerant than most of a President who cheats on his wife and lies about it.

Regular patrons of Burger King headed the list of Clinton's supporters with 79 percent, followed by users of Apple Computer (67 percent), a product which, Dimassimo explains, 'could have died several times over, the brand that people love despite its business weaknesses'.

It is, in large part, a brand's ability to trigger certain such emotional responses that provides it with a winning edge over less familiar products and services. As AOL executive Bob Pittman remarked:

> *I remind people all the time that Coca-Cola does not win the taste test. Microsoft is not the best operating system. Brands win.*

Choice of brands, and a readiness to try a newcomer to the market, therefore depends on the extent to which the personality that has developed around that product or service is liked because consumers see it as being in some way like themselves. If the brand's 'personality' comes across as unlike our own we are less likely to buy it. The sort of 'personality' that a brand develops depend largely on the stories that advertisers and marketers decide to weave around it.

Authenticity, Credibility and Expertise

There are exceptions to the general rule that liking, authenticity and credibility are highly correlated. Indeed, paradoxically, circumstances can even arise in which being intensely disliked can enhance credibility. Some years ago, for example, a friend of mine was involved in a lawsuit and asked me to go with him when he met the barrister who would handle his case in court. The man was exceedingly rude to my friend, taking him through a nerve-racking cross-examination and treating him with barely disguised contempt. As we stumbled out of chambers, numb from the shock of the encounter, I asked my friend whether he still intended to use the barrister.

'Absolutely,' he replied enthusiastically. 'Anyone that disagreeable can only have risen so high in his profession by being absolutely brilliant! Besides which,' he added thoughtfully, 'if he can be that unpleasant to his client, think what he'll do to the opposition!'

The extent to which expertise can override personal dislike for an individual was demonstrated in a 1991 study by Roobina Ohanian, associate professor of marketing at Emory University.[10] She studied the extent to which celebrities influence consumers' intention to purchase various products, using the examples of John McEnroe (promoting tennis rackets), Tom Selleck (men's cologne), Madonna (designer jeans) and Linda Evans (perfume).

The results, shown in the graphs opposite, indicate how significantly liking and credibility go together. But also notice that even though John McEnroe received low scores on trustworthiness and physical attraction, two key elements of liking, his ratings soared on expertise. This gave his commercials one of the highest 'intention to purchase' ratings of all four celebrities.

Credibility, authenticity and granfalloons

Novelist Kurt Vonnegut coined the term 'Granfalloons' to describe the groups with whom we most readily identify. Some we are born into, the most important of these being our family; others we choose to identify

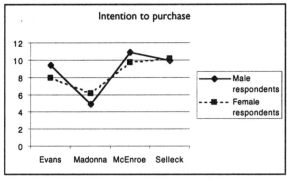

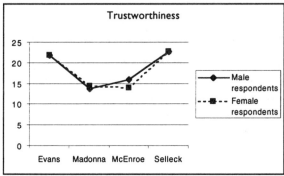

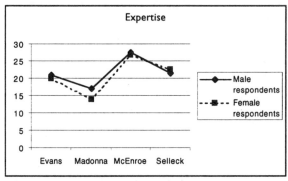

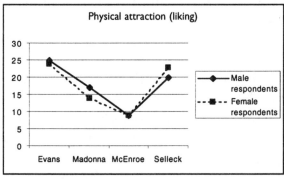

with, although in making this choice we are often strongly influenced by the Granfalloons to which we already belong. Being a member of a large family, for example, may make us more attracted by other groups, such as athletic or sports teams, than an only child would be. The greater our sense of identity with an individual or group, the more likely we are to wear its symbols and the more protective we will be if it ever comes under attack from outsiders. This strength of feeling is, curiously, unconnected with how we became involved with that particular Granfalloon in the first place.

Even when our reasons for belonging to a particular group are unclear or meaningless to us, we will still identify with the group. In one study, when complete strangers were assigned to a particular group on the toss of a coin, they rapidly developed a strong sense of identification with other group members.

This means that any product or brand that we associate with an important Granfalloon in our life – our family, our sports team or our peer group, for instance – will be seen as both likeable and credible. Those associated with a rival Granfalloon, on the other hand, may be disliked and distrusted purely on the basis of that association.

An example of commercial Granfalloons is given by the purchase circles set up by internet bookseller Amazon.com. These enable readers to discover the type of books that people living in their town or city, their place of work or their college are reading. Purchase circles are created by applying a mathematical formula to anonymous data derived from domain names and zip codes. This produces a list of bestsellers within a specific Granfalloon, such as New York City, Oracle Corporation or the Harvard Business School, rather than reflecting the buying habits of the public at large.

The assumptions we make about liking or disliking, trusting or distrusting, a person or product on the basis of their perceived attitudes and attributes are just that – assumptions based on the particular window through which one of our important Granfalloons views the world. This, in turn, relates to each individual's tastespace, a crucial marketing concept in the New Economy and one that I shall examine in detail in Chapter 4.

The message for manufacturers and advertisers is clear. If New Consumers like your company and the products or services it provides, they are more likely to treat as credible any statements you make and more likely to view your products and services as authentic. They are also far more likely to demonstrate genuine, as opposed to pseudo, loyalty towards your business, a topic I shall discuss more fully in Chapter 9.

Authenticity and Story Telling

We live in an age in which more stories are being told, by more story-tellers, to a greater number of people and over vaster distances than at any other time. Some of these stories are entirely true, many are utterly false, with the vast majority probably somewhere between the two.

There is nothing new in mankind being entertained, informed, guided and persuaded by stories. Indeed, as Joseph Campbell points out in his book *Creative Mythology*:

> *The rise and fall of civilisations in the long, broad course of history can be seen to have been largely a function of the integrity and cogency of their supporting canons of myth; for not authority but aspiration is the motivator, builder and transformer of civilisations.*

Unlike the stories of the past, however, many modern tales are woven around a product or service that offers the listener an instant and easily affordable transformation – the physical means to turn that story into reality by making its outcome part and parcel of the listener's personal experience.

One of the first to recognize and exploit this crucial element of modern commercial story telling was Shirley Polykoff, a junior copywriter for the advertising agency Foote, Cone & Belding. The year was 1956 and Clairol was about to launch the first ever product that enabled women to lighten, tint, condition and shampoo their hair in a single step and in their own homes.

When she was handed the account, Shirley Polykoff recalled an incident that had occurred when a boyfriend had taken her home to meet his mother. The woman had stared suspiciously at her hair for a moment, then demanded of her son: 'Does she dye her hair?'

Shirley was one of only 7 percent of American women who did dye her hair and that question had hurt, because at the time there was considerable stigma attached to doing so. Like premarital sex, it was just not something nice girls did! But, thinking about her experience in the light of the new account, she decided to incorporate those suspicions into a story she would weave around coloring one's hair. A 'girl next door' type would be photographed with two people staring at her and demanding: 'Does she or doesn't she?'

The essence of the story was that, thanks to Clairol, authentic hair color could be so easily and convincingly faked that not even the man who was embracing you would know the difference. It was a powerful tale and one that, during the 20 years Polykoff worked on the account, increased the proportion of American women who colored their hair to 40 percent and transformed hair dye into a billion-dollar industry.

But Polykoff's story, although successful on many levels, had an implicit downside. 'You can achieve whatever you want to achieve through subterfuge' ran the subtext, raising a question – if you do succeed in this way, how will you ever know whether it was you or the fakery that made a difference?

By the 1970s the growing power of New Consumers, who wanted to make it on their own terms rather than as a result of trickery, meant that a different type of story was needed. In 1973, while working on the L'Oréal Preference account, Ilon Specht, a 23-year-old copywriter at the McCann-Erikson advertising agency in New York, provided just that.

Ilon recalls the moment when the story came to her very clearly. With four weeks to the copy deadline and no clear idea of the direction the campaign should take, an urgent meeting had been called. Ilon sat and listened while those around her, all males and all far more experienced in advertising than she was, discussed their ideas. The more she listened the angrier she became:

I could just see that they had this traditional view of women, and my feeling was that I'm not writing an ad about looking good for men, which is what it seems to me that they were doing. I just thought, Fuck you. I sat down and did it, in five minutes. It was very personal. I can recite to you the whole commercial, because I was so angry when I wrote it.[11]

The slogan Ilon came up with was: 'Because I'm worth it.'

Today, seven out of ten American women associate that message with L'Oréal. For a brand name this would be remarkable – for an advertising slogan it is almost without precedent.

Shirley Polykoff and Ilon Specht had, between them, developed a genre of commercial story telling that – for the first time – took into account the psychology of consumption. It recognized that if you are going to persuade consumers, especially New Consumers, to buy something, you must weave around the product or service a story that not only has emotional appeal but also communicates an authentic message. That remains as true in the New Economy as it did when Polykoff first put pen to paper.

Indeed, one of the great ironies in an age of unprecedented technological advance is that human emotions continue to play a paramount role in the commercial success of many products and services. Says Rolf Jensen in *The Dream Society*:

> *Profit will be generated by the emotional content of the product itself. Companies will become story owners rather than product owners and they will be able to graft new products on to existing stories.*

Telecommunications firms, for example, could be in the business of weaving stories about 'friendship and love', as illustrated by British Telecom, whose advertising focuses on strengthening social and family bonds.

Mechanical digger company Caterpillar sells rugged shoes on the back of its 'tough' work story, Marlboro man's story has moved away from cigarettes to include a range of clothing, while Body Shop customers buy its convictions along with its products.

Within a decade, Jensen predicts, there could be some 5000 story-owning companies. But in order to impress and persuade, the stories must overcome an initial hurdle that has confronted every storyteller throughout history. You first need to attract the attention of listeners and then convince them your tale is so fascinating, important and personally relevant that they should to take the time to listen. The problem for modern tale tellers is that both attention and time are in shorter supplier than they have ever been and the competition for small amounts of either is correspondingly fiercer.

In Chapter 3 I shall be examining the scarcities of the New Economy in more detail and suggesting practical ways to win a fair share of both.

Authenticity – Your Company's Passport to Prosperity

Over the next decade companies producing only commodities may find themselves struggling to survive in a marketplace increasingly dominated by intense global competition and falling prices, while those able to satisfy the New Consumers' appetite for authenticity will flourish.

For example, the New Consumer's drive for authenticity even extends to television viewers' appetite for shows featuring 'authentic' (i.e. real) people, which has led to the international success of 'castaway' programs such as *Big Brother* and *Survivor*, or *Who Wants to Be a Millionaire?*, a quiz show with an almost unique minimalist style that focuses on the contestant and their reactions as they win or lose large amounts of money.

There are five routes that manufacturers and service providers can take in order to invest their products with the imprimatur of authenticity.

Route one: Locate your product in place

By laying claim to a particular location, companies can often acquire an authenticity for their products or services that is denied to competing brands, even when these are apparently identical. Examples are Swiss watches, French wines, Scottish single malt whisky, Dutch cheese, Thai silk and Spanish leather goods.

Tap water drawn from an anonymous reservoir is a rootless commodity that attracts no premium. Bottled water, by contrast, commands a high price simply by being drawn from a location claimed to endow it with special properties. Evian, for example, promotes itself as originating in the French Alps, where it is produced 'by snow and rain slowly filtering through mineral-rich glacial formations'. The result is an authentic and much sought after drink served in the best restaurants.

Choosing the right location for products or services is by no means a trivial matter, since in many cases it can make the difference between success and failure. Howard Schultz firmly located Starbucks in Milan, capital city of the coffee culture.

Route two: Locate your product in time

Products rooted in a specific era are likely to be viewed as authentic, even if at the time of their manufacture they were merely commodities. The period itself is less important than the association, and can range anywhere from antique (more than a century old) to *avant garde*. All that matters is for the link to a specific period to be established and to appear credible. As New Consumers have become ever more influential in the marketplace, so too has the value of even the recent past.

In entertainment and music, the fifties, sixties, seventies and even eighties have been revived and some major events, such as the music festival Woodstock, have been recreated to satisfy the demand for authenticity. Many of the biggest box office movies of the last 10 years, for example, have been new versions of old television shows, such as *Batman*, *Lost in Space*, *Mission Impossible*, *The Flintstones* and *Star Trek*.

The value of time as an authenticity marker is also reflected in the explosion over the last decade of retro styles and fashions. In the US, one of the most remarkable retail phenomena of recent years has been the success of Restoration Hardware stores, founded by Stephen Gordon. Its 65 stores nationwide stock such nostalgia-inducing items as Jumbo Jerry floursack towels, from a 'thrifty era, when sometimes making do meant making sense', to clockwork tinplate Atomic Robots from the sixties. Himself a passionate enthusiast of times past, Stephen Gordon describes his retail outlets as 'point-of-view' stores, and stocks the shelves with things he personally values, from Tiburon teak steamer chairs to the 'original 1955 Duncan yo-yo'. The one element linking these disparate items and creating a hot line from heartstrings to purse strings is – of course – authenticity.

Route three: Make your product credible

As I have already mentioned, New Consumers tend to be much less trusting than Old ones. Since they are more suspicious of authority in general, simply being told that something is the case fails to impress them. They want to be given concrete evidence that things are as they are claimed to be before judging them either credible or unreliable. Old Consumers, by contrast, tend to require a less rigorous standard of proof before accepting such claims.

For both groups the credibility of the source is of paramount importance when judging authenticity, the difference lying mainly in which sources are regarded as credible. Old Consumers might regard a claim made in a supermarket tabloid as entirely credible, although it would probably be dismissed – or at least viewed with deep suspicion – by New Consumers. The latter, on the other hand, could find similar claims in the *New York Times* or *The Economist* entirely credible, since these are seen as authentic sources of accurate information.

A few major companies have CEOs whose faces and exploits spill over from the business press into the pages of *Hello* and *OK!* Virgin's Richard Branson's ballooning exploits, Microsoft's Bill Gates' lavish new mansion and The Body Shop's Anita Roddick's expeditions to remote jungles in the quest for new products have launched thousands of column inches. These high-profile CEOs can lend credibility and authenticity to a product only so long as they themselves are regarded as both. But let them fall from public favor, and that once profitable visibility then works against the company.

Route four: Make your product original

When Matt Groening created the television cartoon *The Simpsons* he deliberately chose an odd color scheme to make the show stand out from the crowd. Channel-hopping viewers quickly become desensitized by the 'sameness' of the shows, which then come to be regarded as commodities. *The Simpsons*, with its gaudy mix of yellow characters in multicolored settings, is sufficiently original to grab viewers' attention and to be regarded as an authentic work of art.

Even the most commonplace and functional of products can be endowed with authenticity if sufficient skill goes into their design and manufacture. In the 1980s low-priced watches were regarded as commodities purchased simply to keep track of the time. Industry leaders Citizen and Seiko had cornered the market by using quartz movements to improve accuracy and digital displays to make them easier to read. Because all watches were roughly the same, and served only the single, practical purpose of time telling, few people bothered to own more than one of them.

The Swiss, whose traditional clockwork watch movements had been savaged by the influx of these budget-price competitors, decided to hit back by introducing something truly original, the designer watch or Swatch. Swiss parent company SMH established a center in Italy, which was given the brief to create a watch combining powerful technology with brilliant colors and flamboyant designs. The originality and eye appeal of Swatches made them an instant hit, especially among New Consumers who viewed them as fashion accessories and bought several.

Route five: Make your product fun

Increasingly, products that offer a strong element of entertainment, that convey a sense of excitement, that are intriguing and include a touch of showbiz flair, will storm to the top of the New Consumer's 'must have' list.

'There's no business without show business,' claims Michael J. Wolf, a senior partner at the Booz-Allen & Hamilton thinktank. 'Marketers,' he wrote in Forbes ASAP, 'must now engage, inform, titillate, captivate ... in a word they must be fun.'[12]

Recent examples of highly successful products with the fun factor range from the strictly utilitarian, such as the revamped Volkswagen

Beetle and the ice blue Mac, to the unashamedly bizarre, including Billy the Bass, a singing fish that belts out 'Don't Worry, Be Happy' and 'Take Me to the River' – more than a million were sold in the UK in less than six months.

Summary

◆ New Consumers are seeking authenticity in most of their major purchases, whether of products, services or experiences.

◆ New Consumers are attracted by authenticity not just because it seems to offer superior quality, but because ownership of the authentic helps bridge a perceived gulf between their real and ideal selves.

◆ The emphasis on consumerism in society has led many to develop feelings of alienation, which they seek to overcome via spirituality and/or shopping.

◆ Authenticity is a function of the story woven around a product or service. Those with a powerful, relevant and compelling story to tell will win big in the New Economy, while companies whose stories are either non-existent, uninteresting or irrelevant are set to fail.

◆ Although judgments about what is and isn't authentic are frequently subjective, there are five routes that manufacturers and marketers can follow to endow products with authenticity.

◆ This can be done by locating them in a specific place or a particular period of time, by making them original, by being credible and/or by possessing great expertise and by making them fun.

◆ Credibility may be provided by a charismatic individual, a well-managed organization or the manner in which a service is provided. Recognizing a New Consumer's individuality can be sufficient to transform a mundane commercial encounter into an authentic experience.

3

The New Scarcities of Time, Attention and Trust

I've become convinced that our society now consists of only two classes of people. It's not a divide by birthright. It's a divide by time. There are large numbers of people who spend huge amounts of time to save money, and a small group of people who spend huge amounts of money to save time.

Dr Peter Cochrane, Frontiers

Shortly before midnight on every new leap year, a secret club of Oxford professors gathers and, as the clock strikes midnight, they all start walking backwards in an effort to stop time! There is, of course, absolutely no reason for time to stop in its tracks, nor do the professors really believe it will. The ceremony is merely an ancient and eccentric tradition. New Consumers, by contrast, are not merely *attempting* to hold back time, in some cases they are succeeding, using a variety of strategies to warp it for their own convenience.

In these sometimes desperate attempts to squeeze an even greater number of activities into the 168 hours available in any one week, New Consumers are driven not by choice but by necessity. Time, attention and trust are the scarcities of the New Economy and exist not in the marketplace itself but within New Consumers themselves.

Although each scarcity is separate and distinct, they are also inextricably linked. Shortages of time inevitably result in reduced spans of attention and this, in turn, makes New Consumers less trusting. First, they are either unwilling or unable to invest sufficient time in developing a close relationship with suppliers. Second, time pressures make them less tolerant of any delays or errors on the part of their suppliers. Finally, intense competition means they are continually being tempted by better offers from rival firms.

In this chapter we shall be examining these scarcities in detail to reach an understanding of how they arise, how they affect New Consumers and how they influence many purchasing decisions.

Scarcities of Time

For the greater part of human history, life was regulated by the sun and the seasons. The pace was slow and measures of time tended to be haphazard and imprecise. In Medieval Europe, the church regulated time and canonical 'hours' referred not to periods of 60 minutes but to less precise parts of the day set aside for prayer: Matins before dawn, Prime at sunrise and None at nine. None was later advanced to midday, giving us 'noon'.

Although mechanical clocks were invented as early as the fourteenth century, for centuries they remained little more than status symbols rather than being a means of telling the time. In an agricultural society where work patterns were dictated by the length of the day and the seasons of the year, there was little need to measure time with accuracy. As late as the seventeenth century, sundials and church bells were the main way for the general public to regulate their days. The word 'clock' itself comes from *clocca*, the Latin for 'bell'.

Puritan opposition to the Roman Catholic ecclesiastical calendar led to the development of a more modern attitude towards time, and by the start of the eighteenth century the idea of a six-day working week followed by a day of rest had become widely accepted. In 1784, John

Palmer, MP for Bath, created Britain's first public transport system, running to a timetable. He organized a series of stage coaches that left Bath in the late afternoon and reached the Lombard Street general post office in the City of London by eight o'clock the following morning.

When the service was first introduced UK towns and cities set their clocks by local or sun time. As a result, a town in the west of England might be 20 minutes behind London, while one in the east was seven minutes ahead. To take account of these local time changes, Palmer's coaches carried timepieces set to lose or gain as required.

The Industrial Revolution began to move humanity from natural to machine time. The need to transport goods, materials and people around the country at low cost and higher speeds than could be achieved by horse and carriage led to the construction of railway networks throughout Europe and North America. Even after these links were established, however, attitudes towards time remained casual. In 1839, when George Bradshaw was compiling the first ever railway timetable, one company refused to provide him with any arrival times, on the grounds that 'It would tend to make punctuality a sort of obligation'!

After the completion in 1856 of St Stephen's Tower, containing London's most famous bell, Big Ben (named after boxer Benjamin Caunt, who weighed 238lbs at his last fight), the astronomer royal, Sir George Airy, insisted that its clocks be set to Greenwich Mean Time. All Britain's clocks shortly followed suit.

In industrial towns and cities, a giant clock above the mill or factory often kept time for an entire community. Bosses were not above ensuring that these ran more slowly during the working day and speeded up once the factory had closed. To avoid the deception being revealed, employees were forbidden to bring their own pocket watches on to the premises. From this comes the tradition of presenting a retiring worker with a watch or clock to symbolize that time was finally his or her own.

By the dawn of the twentieth century, time was becoming increasingly regulated throughout the world's industrialized nations. The invention of the 'consumer' as a distinct role during the industrial era was accompanied by a speeding up of everyday tasks. Industrial life required synchronization of behavior in mass production and mass leisure pursuits.

In America the time and motion studies developed by industrial engineer Frederick E. Taylor made the productive use of time an ever more urgent issue for managers and workforce alike. Everyone had to conform to this accelerated lifecycle, with workers following machine-like routines in order to eliminate unnecessary movements.

Today we are living in an accelerating age. Instead of new fashions taking months to spread, they can now leap instantaneously from one side of the planet to the other. News of all kinds has become a source of immediate observation, if not revelation. As the Gulf War showed, cameras can bring the heat of battle into the front room even as the shells are flying. Journeys that would once have taken weeks or months braving discomforts and dangers may now be accomplished in a matter of hours in safety and comfort.

Electronic communications, e-commerce, conference calls and tele-conferencing allow 'meetings' with people on the other side of the world to occur in real time. The speed of communication also means that bad news travels as fast, sometimes even faster, than good. Twenty years ago the fallout from a boom or bust in any of the world's stock or currency markets took days or weeks to make its reverberations felt on a global scale. In today's digitally networked world, repercussions are felt almost instantaneously, as the Asian financial crisis of 1998 showed.

New Consumers are developing such a need for speed that, for many, time itself is perceived as passing more rapidly. In a recent study we stopped people in London and New York and asked them to esti-mate how long it took for 30 seconds to pass. Eight out of ten Londoners and nine out of ten New Yorkers significantly under-estimated how long that half minute took to pass, with New Yorkers seeing time as passing even faster than Londoners. On New York's Fifth Avenue one in five thought 30 seconds went by in less than 15, while in London's Oxford Street the proportion was one in seven.

There are four main reasons for time becoming so scarce that we are all having to run twice as fast in today's highly paced global market-place. The first, and most obvious, is that many people simply have too much to do.

So much to do

Downsizing during the 1980s and pressures to keep down costs, combined with intense competition, mean that many of us are working longer hours than in the recent past, while urban traffic congestion adds to the delays for those commuting to and from the office or paying business calls by car.

In the office, workers are facing time pressures from the ever-increasing amounts of information with which they have to deal on a daily basis – not only paper reports, letters and faxes, but electronic correspondence as well. 'I answer all my letters, read all my memos, deal with all the other paperwork and then switch on my computer to find 200 e-mails awaiting my urgent attention,' one manager told us despondently.

An international survey conducted by Reuters in the late 1990s, which examined the issue of information overload among executives in the UK, the US, Australia, Hong Kong and Singapore, found that in order to deal with the sheer volume of information crossing their desks in an average week, half (49 percent) regularly stayed late and took work home at the weekends.[1] Despite such pressures, however, a majority of executives (85 percent) felt it imperative to obtain as much information as possible in order to keep pace with the opposition.

More time is also being spent on shopping for basics; including travel this has risen from around 40 minutes a day in 1961 to 80 minutes at the start of the millennium.

In the home, as one might expect, the vast array of labor-saving gadgets now available – including washing machines, dishwashers, microwaves, blenders and vacuum cleaners – has freed a certain amount of the time previously spent on domestic chores. Yet even in the best-equipped homes such savings seldom amount to more than 30 minutes a day. Just as Parkinson's law dictates that office work will expand to fill the time available, so domestic work increases in proportion to the number of machines on hand to tackle it. Washing machines, for example, have encouraged us to launder our clothes daily instead of weekly, so generating seven times as much washing and ironing. Similarly, now that the daily shower has replaced the weekly bath, the time devoted to washing has risen from 30 minutes a week to more than two hours.

Since time has to be found from somewhere to meet these additional demands, the one thing most usually sacrificed is sleep. Research by the American National Sleep Foundation discovered that a third (32 percent) of Americans – many of whom, according to recent figures from the International Labour Organisation, now work the longest hours in the world – enjoy fewer than six hours' sleep a night. 'We seem to be getting about 90 minutes less sleep a night than people did a century ago,' says sleep specialist Peter Martin.

The result is a sleep debt, which can have profound effects on our ability to carry out some tasks efficiently. Mental processes start to slow: losing only four hours sleep in one night can reduce a person's reaction time by up to 45 percent. One's capacity for focusing on a specific task is greatly reduced. The mind starts to wander and mistakes are made. Memory is impaired, as are logical reasoning abilities. In *Sleep Thieves* professor of psychology Stanley Coren comments:

> As sleep debt increases, we act more and more like a machine or an aeroplane on autopilot. Anything out of the ordinary will cause us to start to make errors.

As a result, further time has to be spent correcting the mistakes made on earlier attempts due to fatigue. Even when people enjoy sufficient sleep, time pressures can lead to stress. In the survey cited above, more than 80 percent of executives regarded their workplace as stressful to some extent, while four in ten described it as extremely stressful every day. What is more, nine in ten (94 percent) of managers do not believe their situation will improve. As with fatigue, excessive stress leads to poorer performance, resulting in mistakes and errors that require more expenditure or precious time to put right.

Increasing commercial competition

Advances in computer technology and telecommunications mean that every process of a sale is speeded up. Production is faster due to the ease of connecting to suppliers, and thanks to the low-cost, global nature of the internet, markets can be found more rapidly than ever before.

During the 1960s when the first generation of business computers, mostly mainframes, came on line, business cycles lasted from 10 to 15 years. This shrank to between five and eight years with the arrival of minicomputers in the 1980s and fell further to between twelve months and two years in the 1990s as client/server systems became more widespread. Today some industries, including personal computers, have seen their cycles shrink to six months.

Business decisions must be lightning fast to take account of the speed with which electronic markets move. In many spheres of commercial activity, where obtaining information even a fraction of a second before the competition can mean the difference between reward and ruin, only two types of organization can now exist – the quick and the dead. Fortune no longer merely favors the bold, it bestows even greater benefits on the swift. Perhaps because New Consumers now take instantaneous information for granted, many have also come to expect products and services to be delivered almost as rapidly.

Management guru Tom Peters recalls how when he was working at McKinsey and Co, inflation was never even taken into account while making 20-year cashflow projections for quarter-billion-dollar petrochemical facilities. It was believed that supply, demand and commodity prices for wheat and corn could be predicted with a fine degree of accuracy over this period. Peters now considers that 'if you aren't reorganizing pretty substantially once every 6 to 12 months, you're probably out of step with the times'.

In large part this exponential rate of change is being driven by the astonishing quantities of information being produced in the New Economy. The sheer volume of this information – the weekday edition of the *New York Times*, for example, contains more information than the average seventeenth-century citizen would have come across in a lifetime[2] – presents us with further pressures on our time, to such an extent that it has become impossible for any individual to keep up with more than a tiny fraction of the total new information available in almost any field of research or study. Each day some 20 million words of technical information are recorded. As author Hubert Murray Jr. points out:

> *A reader capable of reading 1,000 words per minute would require 1.5 months, reading eight hours every day, to get through one day's output, and at the end of that period he would have fallen 5.5 years behind in his reading.*[3]

Bill Gates, in his book *Business @ the Speed of Thought*, describes how the forces of digital information have brought about a commercial environment in which the only constant is change: 'Evolutionists would call this punctuated chaos – constant upheaval marked by brief respites.'

These commercial pressures make such demands on New Consumers' time that they only rarely enjoy the luxury of stepping back, taking stock and reflecting on their next move. Eventually the relentless pressure can lead to physical illness or intellectual burnout. For many the only answer is downshifting, accepting a lower income in return for a more relaxed outcome. One financial director who opted for early retirement in his mid-fifties and went to run a small farm told us: 'I no longer want to handle any timeframe shorter than a season.'

Increasing social competition inside and outside the workplace

With the erosion of job security, many employees now find themselves in direct competition with their work colleagues, resulting in greater pressure to work overtime at the office or put in extra hours at the evenings and weekends.

In a growing number of companies, 'team players' are seen as those whose car is first into the carpark each morning and last to leave at night. In one company a senior manager walks around the carpark at 7.30 am and feels the radiator of every vehicle – those still warm earn a black mark on the personnel file of their owners.

In a work world where the fear of being overtaken by ambitious colleagues keeps many chained to their desks, acts of deception are practiced that in a less fraught context would seem laughably childish. Some US office workers, for example, advance the times shown on their e-mails before surreptitiously leaving by a rear entrance. One New York banking executive is reported to bribe security guards with hot stock tips in return for their looking the other way as he creeps from the building around 7.30 each evening.

These pressures have led to a culture in some organizations that management expert Charles Handy terms 'presenteeism': the belief that physically being in the workplace for more hours gives the impression of being hard working. While these 'empty suits', to use another expression of Handy's, contribute nothing but their presence, they are often looked on favorably by managers who expect to be able to squeeze as many waking hours as possible from their workforce.

Outside work, advertising and the consumption ethic encourage people to compare themselves with those on higher incomes, creating desires that are beyond their means to support. Single parents, for instance, often find themselves under great pressure from their children to provide them with the same sort of possessions found in two-income households.

During the late 1950s, at the height of Old Consumer power, people tended to compare themselves with their neighbors, striving to 'keep up with the Joneses'. Today, when many urban dwellers know little or nothing about those living around them, role models are more likely to be drawn from high-income 'reference groups'. These may be more senior people at work, those met socially or even characters from popular TV shows. Despite being merely creations of a scriptwriter's imagination, the latter often set the benchmark for spending 'norms', creating ever-rising standards of expectations among those attempting to emulate them. Purchased on credit, such expenditure must often be paid for in time – overtime.

Less family division of labor

The decline of the traditional family means that those living alone or as single parents are obliged to take on tasks that might previously have been shared. In 1960 just over a quarter of married women aged 25 to 34 in the US had a job; today that proportion has risen to more than 70 percent. This means that a majority of women are now working two shifts, one in the office or factory and a second at home, spending time that might otherwise have been used for socializing, enjoying a leisure pursuit or just winding down.

Time warps

These four factors combine to devour time, reducing – sometimes to zero – the amount available for personal pursuits. As a result, the pressure for many people is not just intense but relentless.

'Time,' claimed Oscar Wilde, 'is a waste of money.' Many New Consumers would agree and are continually looking for ways to save both by devising means for warping time to meet the demands they must make on it. Seven such timewarps are widely used.

Timewarp one: Living in the fast lane

The director of NASA, Daniel Goldin, has a simple motto for his space program: 'Faster, smaller, cheaper, better.' The New Consumer has an identical attitude, with the emphasis on 'faster'. In order to complete as many tasks as possible in the course of a day or a week, they expect things to happen fast and to finish quickly, allowing them to move directly to the next task or challenge.

Studies have shown that the speed of life varies between town and country, and even from one city to the next. In urban environments, people not only walk and talk faster, they are also far less patient of delays. As a result a host of schemes, from fast-food eateries to ATMs, have grown up to help hard-pressed consumers warp time still further. The communications industry depends for its prosperity on our perceived need to make instant contact with one another, any time, any place, anywhere. As consumer specialist Burton Brodo commented:

> *Yesterday there was urgency, yet we waited to get to a 'pay' telephone to make that 'important' call. Today we instantly dial up our cellular phone wherever we happen to be. In the past we might be content to wait for two or three days for a document to arrive via the mail – now this same document must be 'faxed' immediately.*

That comment was made before the widespread use of e-mail, which has reduced still further the time taken between origination, dissemination and assimilation.

Instead of wading through piles of business magazines and books, many executives subscribe to abridgment services that gut articles and texts to identify the key issues and condense them into reports that can be read in minutes. Rapid reading courses are also popular, with one bestselling program claiming that it will allow you to read 25,000 words a minute, a promise many time-starved New Consumers would find irresistible.

New Consumers also conform far less to pressures for communal time – those periods when mass audiences view a television show simultaneously or all go on vacation during the same two weeks of the year.

'We'll all live very asynchronous lives, in far less lockstep obedience to each other,' comments digital technologist Nicholas Negroponte, who believes that in the very near future, 'prime time will be my time'.

Timewarp two: Accelerating business

In 1959 scientist and novelist C.P. Snow argued that the humanities and the sciences represented 'two cultures' that failed to communicate adequately and frequently failed to understand one another. Today, the New Consumer is responsible for an even greater cultural division – that between the fast and the slow. Because fast nations, fast corporations and fast individuals produce more in the same amount of time as their slower counterparts, they are individually and collectively capable of earning more per hour.

The onset of the Information Age and the emergence of the New Consumer have stepped up the speed with which events occur. Put simply, because more intelligence is applied to work, more can be done, or a higher quality of products delivered, within a shorter period. And more businesses are faced with the choice of either adopting time-warping innovations or losing out to the competition.

Speed increases in the information age have largely been due to the use of 'dumb' intelligence, so called because the intelligence manifested is an emergent property of the system rather than an organizing principle.

Dumb intelligence is found in two types of system, connected and automated. Connected networks of travel and communications, such as railways, roads, telephones and the internet, function more intelligently as a result of the very act of connection. Imagine the problems and delays of traveling along stretches of road or rail that didn't connect with any other roads or railway lines. Similarly, linking computers into nets means the whole becomes more powerful than the sum of its parts. In fact, the value of a network increases by the square of the individual nodes (units) involved.

Automated systems are standardized methods for doing a job that can be programmed into a computer or a robot or – as Frederick Taylor's time and motion studies showed – taught to a human worker without demanding an especially high level of skill.

Taylor broke complex tasks down into their constituent actions, determined which of these were essential and discarded any that were not. In some cases he would advocate that the labor be divided among a number of workers with certain tasks, such as sharpening tools, delegated to specialists.

As the Information Age began to require round-the-clock and round-the-globe services, companies were obliged to automate a great many skills in order to provide the consistently high standards of service or product quality, at the speed demanded by time-starved New Consumers, irrespective of where or when they made their purchase.

Passengers expect the same level of safety and service from a reputable airline no matter what time of day or night they catch their flight and no matter where in the world they happen to be. Such consistency can only be achieved by standardizing the tasks involved as far as possible by establishing systems, protocols and checklists.

Sociologist Anthony Giddens uses the terms 'disembedding mechanisms' to describe the ways in which automation decouples skills from individuals and makes them generally available.

While automation and connectivity are allowing New Consumers to warp time more effectively, there is a downside for companies racing to be first past the post. Thinking and acting at high speed gives employees a perspective on life significantly different to that of those able to perform at a more leisurely pace. And since slower companies and individuals are now in the minority this can, ironically, allow them to do things that fast-paced companies and individuals are unable to achieve.

Enterprises that move more cautiously are exposed to fewer risks of failure from brand new products or services, placing them in the enviable position of having a uniquely elevated perspective. By waiting to evaluate how a market reacts they are able to develop a more informed strategy for their own entrance into the market.

The different perspective enjoyed by those who are slow may also lead them to new insights that the faster-acting individuals and organisations may miss. It could also help them to be more creative.

'One of the great paradoxes and madnesses of this age,' says Tom Peters, 'is that we don't have significant doses of time to be creative. Intensity does not breed creativity.'

Timewarp three – Buying on credit

Old Consumers often waited patiently and saved hard for high-ticket purchases like cars or furniture. New Consumers can warp time by making purchases before they have the financial means to do so. With credit becoming ever more easily available to most consumers for purchasing virtually anything, they are able to 'live now, pay later', without effort. Many banks even promote the idea of taking out a second mortgage in order to enjoy an exotic holiday or a luxury sports car.

In the US alone there are more than five million credit card-reading devices; worldwide there are nearly 400 million Visa cards being used for 7.9 billion transactions a year. This has meant a great shift in attitudes towards the gratification of 'wants', which are no longer seen as something that has to be postponed but a pleasure to enjoy almost instantly.

Timewarp four: Shopping around the clock

As pressure on time increases, New Consumers are demanding ways of spending their money when and where they want to. Home shopping via catalogs, TV shopping channels and the internet saves the time that would otherwise be spent traveling to and from retailers. Internet and telephone banking not only saves time but also enables banking transactions to be carried out 24 hours a day. Videocassettes, DVDs and digital TV enable viewers not only to choose which programs they want to watch but when they watch them. As business consultant Michael de Kare-Silver comments:

> *Consumers are constantly searching for products or services that help them save time. Shopping electronically once it's made easy may be just what consumers having been waiting for.*[4]

Timewarp five: Multitasking

Commuters and business travelers listen to business tapes on the car stereo, take phone calls and dictate letters on to miniature tape recorders, occupy flight and train time preparing reports on their laptops and discussing strategy with colleagues using mobile and air phones. Such multitasking is becoming an increasingly common and popular way for New Consumers to squeeze a few more precious minutes from each fleeting hour.

When shopping they prefer to have all the products and services they require gathered into so-called need pools, such as supermarkets and malls, with post offices, banks, movie theaters, petrol stations and even churches under one roof. The internet is, of course, the ultimate need pool, where it is possible to buy almost anything without leaving your home.

Timewarp six: Getting it yesterday

New Consumers' demand for up-to-the-minute services and newer, better products is accelerating many markets, especially those based on providing information. Business analysts Stan Davis and Christopher Meyer make the point that product cycles have now speeded up to the point of overlap, with several 'generations' existing simultaneously. The original version of a software product, for example, may be sold at a reduced price besides the latest version at a standard price. At the same time consumers are reading reviews of the next version in the computer press, and perhaps even testing out a beta copy.

In order to meet the growing demand for speed, many companies are transforming their traditional businesses into fast-food-style outlets. Everything from processing films and selling shares to divorcing and marrying is now available in a high-speed format.

'If the 1980s were about quality and the 1990s were about reengineering,' says Bill Gates, 'then the 2000s will be about velocity.'

The 'just-in-time' strategy is now the basis not just of manufacturing but of service companies. It is also the strategy used for the creation of much of the information that New Consumers so promiscuously consume. Increasingly, magazines, books and TV shows are created against such tight deadlines that the quality and accuracy of the information on offer are undermined, making already cynical New Consumers even more sceptical about its value. A journalist visiting an isolated village in the Canadian Northwest was asked by one of the locals how long he planned to stay. Before he could reply, another answered for him: 'One day: newspaper story. Two days: magazine story. Five days: book!'

Timewarp seven: Using experts

New Consumers are often concerned about investing precious time on products or services that fail to meet their expectations – wasting two hours at the cinema watching a movie they hate, or visiting a new holiday destination and discovering that they loathe it. To ensure their time is wisely spent they often turn to experts who tell them what to see, what to read, which radio programs to listen to, which television shows are worth watching, the countries to visit and those to avoid, the restaurants at which they should dine and the best food and wine to eat at home. By substituting another's judgment for their own, they avoid the risk of self-recrimination should the experience fail to give satisfaction.

To allay the terror of time wasting, suppliers are continually seeking new ways to provide reassurance, such as encouraging customer-to-customer recommendations or free 'sneak previews'. They are also looking to create a favorable impression with so-called market mavens, highly influential consumers whose opinions and judgments exert a powerful influence over New Consumers. We shall be discussing their crucial role in purchasing decisions in Chapter 5.

Scarcities of Attention

'Pay attention' we are often urged. Attention has become a currency used by New Consumers in an economy where people with something to sell struggle to be noticed by people who might want to buy. This is an economy in which the true purpose of the great majority of the media, and commercial television in particular, is to deliver the greatest number of eyeballs to the largest number of advertisers.

In their *Encyclopaedia of the New Economy*, John Browning and Spencer Reiss perfectly described the attention economy as a 'marketplace based on the idea that while information is essentially infinite, demand for it is limited by the waking hours in a human day'.

When time scarcity becomes attention shortage

Despite our best efforts and most ingenious timewarps, many of us still spend a large proportion of our working day under intense and often conflicting time pressures. Time starvation also means a poverty of attention, with a result that New Consumers often have an extremely short attention span.

In order to understand more about how time shortages affect attention, we have developed a new model of time perception. Instead of segmenting New Consumers into 'categories', as in traditional marketing practice, we believe it makes more sense to examine how they perceive the passage of time while making purchases:

◆ Are they in a rush or in the mood for leisurely browsing?
◆ Are they bored or stimulated by the prospect of spending their money?

As the New Consumer changes roles through the day, they may pop in and out of these different time perception states and can be thought of as having different identities according to the way they are experiencing time. According to our state, we are more or less attentive to such stimuli as advertising.

Like 'shifts' in a factory, these states are not always defined by the time of day. For this reason we call them 'time shifts', each with its own particular demands and characteristics.

Broadly speaking, there are four main time shifts plus one special category: flow time, occasion time, prime time, leisure time and time to kill.

Flow time

We are in flow time whenever we become so absorbed in an activity that time passes unnoticed. So great is our concentration during these often fairly brief periods that we are completely unaware of anything else in our surroundings. Any advertisement that we find so utterly fascinating and absorbing that it causes us to shift into flow time will be carefully attended to and clearly recalled.

Occasion time

This comprises those special moments in life when something momentous or important occurs: getting married, the birth of a child, a job interview or examination. While these can be highly stressful, the stress may be either pleasurable, for example when going off on holiday, or distressing, such as when taking an important exam. Advertisements most likely to be given our undivided attention in this time shift are those clearly relevant to the occasion, such a wedding gown for a woman who has just got engaged, baby clothes for one who is pregnant, books or tapes with tips on how to pass exams for the student caught up in revision.

Deadline time

We are in this shift while working against the clock to complete some task or when engaged in some important activity that cannot be delayed. It is the worst possible time shift in which to try to catch some-one's attention with a commercial message. They are unlikely to pay it more than the most fleeting attention and to remember little, if any-thing, about what they heard or saw.

Leisure time

This time shift is most often found during the evenings, at weekends or when on holiday. Although, as we shall explain in a moment, attention is diffused rather than focused, people do at least have more time to notice the advertisement provided that they are given sufficiently good reasons for doing so.

Time to kill

The final, special category occurs during those periods when we are waiting for something to happen, such as after arriving early for an appointment or while awaiting the departure of a train or aeroplane.

Sometimes people seek to fill this time productively, for example by reading a business report while waiting to speak to a client. Most of the time, however, hard-pressed New Consumers regard 'time to kill' as a sort of bonus, a period when it does not really matter what you do since such time is not regarded as real. Comments Anthony Giddens:

> *Killed time is bounded off from the rest of an individual's life and, unless something unexpected happens, has no consequences for it.*

People in the time-to-kill state are likely to be a captive audience and, given the locations in which much 'killing time' occurs – airports, rail-way stations, planes, ferry terminals, waiting rooms and so on – should represent an excellent marketing opportunity. The rapid expansion of sales outlets in all these locations is in part evidence of the close relationship between consumers having time to kill and their desire to pass that time enjoyably by spending money.

A fairly recent and ingenious way of capitalizing on the time-to-kill shift is washroom advertising, which is set to boom over the next few years. Already companies as diverse as Unilever, Gillette and Vauxhall are using panels in toilets to promote products ranging from cosmetics and toiletries to pharmaceuticals, finance, computers, drinks and food. Even government and social agencies are finding that washroom advertising can grab the attention of those who might otherwise never bother to spend time on their messages. Specialist agency Outdoor Connections, responsible for much of this advertising, points out that panels in toilets have two main advantages:

> *Not only is the audience often captive and fixated on the wall directly in front, this medium can offer point-of-action communications. It could be argued that from a pub washroom your next action might be to buy a drink, exercise your charm or drive home. So for drink, contraceptive and anti-drink campaigns this medium is located at a point of action. Similarly with washroom ads in shopping centres you are likely to continue purchasing after your visit.*[5]

Time, attention and arousal

In order to attend to anything seriously and carefully, our levels of mental and physical arousal need to be set just right. When these are both very low we typically feel so bored that it becomes almost impossible to attend to anything. This often happens during time to kill. Our mind drifts idly from one topic to the next, and we feel lethargic and disinterested. If watching TV we may channel hop in a desultory manner or stare at a program without really taking in anything that is being said or done.

At the other extreme, when arousal is too high we feel anxious and unsettled, once again unable to pay close attention to anything for very long, but this time because so many urgent thoughts are clamoring for our attention. Recall the way most people read a magazine in the dentist's waiting room, nervously flicking through the pages and rarely devoting much time or attention to any particular article.

Between these extremes we have an ideal level of arousal, the point at which we feel neither bored nor anxious. During flow time people are psychologically balanced in this way, with the result that levels of attention are at a peak.

Since when New Consumers' attention flows so does their desire to make purchases, companies that adjust their messages to take account of these variations are likely to have far more notice taken of them and so generate higher sales. Unfortunately, within all these time shifts the amount of attention available is continuing to diminish.

Catching the attention

The pioneering nineteenth-century psychologist William James, brother of novelist Henry James, described the infant's world as a 'booming, buzzing confusion'. The same could be said about virtually everyone today. We spend our lives moving through a glittering haze of sensory information, with a thousand sirens clamoring to attract our ear and catch our eye. Between waking and sleeping in a single day, you are exposed to such a torrent of information that even if you spent just 60 seconds considering each item it would take you 800 years to attend to it all. As Nobel prize-winning economist Herbert Simon commented:

> *What information consumes is rather obvious. It consumes the attention of all its recipients. Hence a wealth of information creates a poverty of attention.*

Every year US television screens $36 billion worth of advertising, while in the UK around 80 new television commercials appear each week at a cost of some £450 million. In the US alone, Media Register, the nation's top advertising expenditure analysts, monitor some 2350 advertisements per day in magazines and newspapers. And they only look at some 500 of the more than 9000 publications currently available.

'Nowadays we are inundated with products, with advertisements, (and with people)' says Winston Fletcher, chairman of the Delaney Fletcher Slaymaker Delaney and Bozell agency. 'We can probably cope with more than our forefathers could – though even that is unproven – but the percentage of the total is shrinking.'

How do we cope with such vast quantities of information? The simple answer is by ignoring the vast majority of it.

Sometimes our decision not to pay attention is intentional. We toss a piece of junk mail into the trash, channel surf to avoid advertisements and turn over pages containing ads. Most of the time, however, we remain blissfully unaware that the information was even available. Processes low down in the brain filter out 99 percent of data received via our senses long before it reaches the conscious mind.

While reading these words, for example, you have probably taken no notice of information from sensors in the muscles of your legs and lower back. Swing the spotlight of attention on to those parts of your body, however, and you immediately become aware of the chair or the bed that is supporting you, perhaps noticing for the first time a tickle around your left knee.

It is the same with commercial messages. Most pass unnoticed, or are so fleetingly observed that they make little, if any, lasting impact.

Psychologists studying the behavior of motorists traveling to and from work coined the phrase 'commuter amnesia' to describe the fact that between leaving home and arriving at work, little of what happened along the way can be recalled. Unless something out of the ordinary happens, such as witnessing an accident, the whole journey vanishes from our memory the moment we close the car door behind us.

The same kind of blanking out, what might be termed 'information amnesia', occurs for all but a tiny proportion of the information flowing around us during every waking moment. This is especially true of commercial messages. Fifteen years ago two-thirds of US viewers could name at least one TV commercial they had seen during the previous month. Today that proportion has fallen to well below half.

In a society where information is virtually limitless, human attention inevitably becomes the most important commodity of all.

Scarcities of Trust

While New Consumers are neither more nor less trusting in their personal relationships than Old Consumers, they are significantly less likely to offer unquestioning trust to suppliers.

Research by the Henley Centre, for example, has shown that while nine out of ten people will trust their spouse or partner and eight out of ten their children, fewer than a third (27 percent) trust retailers or manufacturers, while just 14 percent trust either the government or advertisers!

Among those New Consumers whose lifestyles are characterized by high expectations and a desire for instant gratification, with quality and value for money taken for granted, trust has become one of the scarcest and most sought-after commodities in the New Economy.

In the past, proprietors of small stores, whose family might have served the same community for generations, were usually known, respected and trusted by their neighbors. As late as 1936, delegates attending the National Wholesale Grocers convention and the New Jersey Retail Grocers Association were assured they had nothing to fear from supermarkets, whose 'narrow appeal to the price buyer limited the size of their market'.

Speaker after speaker disparaged them as 'horse and buggy' outfits with 'cracker barrel storekeeping' run by 'unethical opportunists' whose days were clearly numbered. The executive of one chain of general stores remarked it was 'hard to believe that people will drive for miles to shop for foods and sacrifice the personal service chains have perfected and to which Mrs. Consumer is accustomed'.[6]

As the general stores quickly discovered, they either went into the supermarket business themselves or they went bust. Those with 'the courage of their convictions who resolutely stuck to the corner store philosophy,' comments Harvard Business School professor Theodore Levitt dryly, 'kept their pride but lost their shirts.'

As stores, and communities, grew larger and increasingly impersonal, bonds of trust and loyalty disappeared. Trusting the Jones family who had run the corner shop for as long as anybody could remember was one thing, trusting a giant and anonymous corporation such as Wal-Mart or Tesco another matter entirely.

Nor is bribery, whether in the form of loyalty cards, reward cards or special discounts, any substitute for trust based on personal knowledge and respect. Research that my consultancy conducted on behalf of Air Miles found that two-thirds of supermarket customers are always open to a better offer, while one in five feels no loyalty at all to any particular supplier and views every transaction on its own merits. One in ten regards those who are loyal to a supplier as fools who fail to get the best possible deals, and fewer than one in twenty insists nothing would tempt them away from their regular supplier. Journalist Janet Bush comments:

Time and time again the new, canny breed of consumer has played chicken with retailers and won. When retailers tried to put up prices, sales went down. As soon as prices were cut again, shoppers returned.[7]

Another feature that helps to build customer trust is specialization. This worked at a time when shops tended to sell one type of product and consumers called at the pharmacy to purchase medications, the bank for a loan and shoe shops for a pair of boots. Today, while a minority of stores are still able to use specialization as a means of creating and sustaining trust, in many instances it proves more of a handicap than a help. Time-scarce New Consumers expect to buy as many of their basic needs as possible from a single shop, rather than being forced to visit several.

The main key to achieving continued customer trust, however, was neither local monopoly nor specialization, but simply lack of knowledge on the part of customers. As a theologian once observed, 'When people stop believing in God they do not believe nothing, they believe anything!' Similarly, Old Consumers, who frequently knew little or nothing about consumer matters, were more inclined to trust whatever manufacturers, suppliers and advertisers told them about their products or services.

New Consumers, by contrast, are 'informationally empowered' and considerably more selective about where they spend their hard-earned cash. They compare prices and research quality. They discuss new products with one another, read up on product information and are informed via television, radio and the internet. They consult with expert friends and the market mavens whose role in their busy lives we will explore in Chapter 5. Little that manufacturers and advertisers say is taken on trust.

Scarcities of Time, Attention and Trust Can Only Get Worse

As with any scarce resource in a free market, time, attention and trust, already of considerable commercial value, will soar in value as the power and influence of New Consumers increase still further. Since gaining all three is the first essential step in getting any message across, manufacturers and suppliers that fail to recognize the significance of these new scarcities will end up like the Victorian child, neither seen nor heard.

One increasingly widely adopted technique is to make your message so startling, shocking or controversial that people feel unable to ignore it. In May 1999, for example Bartle Bogle Hegarty PR promoted a feature on the 100 sexiest women, for men's magazine *FHM*, by projecting giant images of a nude cover girl on to the side of the House of Commons. This not only attracted the attention of thousands of Londoners but, more importantly, received massive newspaper and television coverage. Clothes retailer Benetton gained international publicity with a series of poster advertisements featuring images ranging from a newborn baby to a man dying of AIDS, while footwear company Candies depicted a woman sitting on a lavatory in advertisements for shoes.

An entirely different approach, advocated by direct marketing guru Seth Godin, is to gain people's *permission* before trying to sell them something, rather than interrupting them with an advertisement while they are trying to do something else, such as watch sport on TV. He notes:

> *Interruption Marketers spend all of their time interrupting strangers. Permission Marketers spend as little time and money*

talking to strangers as they can. Instead, they move as quickly as they can to turn strangers into prospects who choose to 'opt-in' to a series of communications ... Since the prospect has agreed to pay attention, it's much easier to teach them about your product.

Another tactic is to persuade people to take notice of you by paying them for doing so, an approach we shall be examining in detail later.

What all these different approaches have in common is an attempt to break through the scarcity barriers by triggering each consumer's WIIFM, or What's In It For Me? response. Unless time-poor New Consumers are quickly and easily able to recognize the personal payoff for attending to a commercial message, in terms of a meaningful emotional, intellectual or practical reward, they are unlikely to do so.

While some messages have considerable appeal to Old Consumers, such as claims to improve our wellbeing, make us laugh, arouse our curiosity, increase our wealth or give us something for nothing, getting the same message across to cynical, distrusting and time-poor New Consumers requires a more specific and individual approach. In some cases it means identifying their specific areas of interest and targeting your message so that it has direct, personal appeal. Identifying the precise WIIFM factors for a single individual out of millions of consumers might appear an impossible task. Yet it is one that not only can be done but, thanks to the development of retailing technology and computer power, is being done on a regular basis. Based on their history of previous purchases, obtained directly or indirectly from each consumer, it becomes possible to construct a detailed 'map' of personal preferences.

This map of personal preferences is an individual's tastespace. How it can be plotted and why it will provide many companies with their surest method for persuading New Consumers to invest even a little scarce time and attention in their products and services will be explored in Chapter 4.

Summary

◆ Time, attention and trust have become the scarcest resources in the New Economy and companies that fail to recognize this fact are likely to suffer severe financial penalties.

◆ Time scarcities are caused by too many demands being made on our time, increasing global competition, competition within the workplace and less family division of labor. Over the next few years these pressures can only increase, making time and attention even scarcer and so more commercially valuable.

◆ In response to these pressures, consumers are finding various ways of 'warping' time.

◆ Time starvation has led to a second scarcity, of attention. As a result this resource is becoming increasingly valuable and New Consumers, especially, have to be persuaded to invest even a small amount of their limited time in commercial messages.

◆ There are five time shifts, each with a different level of attention associated with it. In order to catch and persuade New Consumers, advertisers need to take notice of the time shift consumers are most likely to be experiencing in different situations.

◆ Attention to a message depends on how effective it is in triggering a WIIFM or 'What's In It For Me?' response among New Consumers. With so many demands being made on their attention, they will only invest in products or services that are clearly offering them something of direct personal relevance and value.

◆ In order to act on the information received, New Consumers need to have trust in both the message and the messenger. Of all the three scarcities, trust is the one in shortest supply. Well-informed New Consumers are generally mistrustful and cynical when it comes to promises and assurances from large and anonymous organizations, whether political parties or commercial concerns.

◆ For many companies the most efficient way of identifying an individual New Consumer's true interests, and so understand more precisely what products and services are likely to possess the greatest appeal, is by through a detailed analysis of each individual's tastespace.

4

Tastespace:
Creating the Ultimate Mall

Buying habits are as individual as fingerprints.
Frank Feather, The Future Consumer

Outside Phoenix, Arizona, is a low-rise building flanked by verdant lawns and surrounded by a chainlink fence, which appears so similar to any of the city's other high-tech office blocks that a casual passerby might easily mistake it for just another corporate headquarters.

Appearances are deceptive.

All the gleaming windows are false and the structure is a concrete iceberg, most of it buried deep beneath the ground. Located directly beneath the Phoenix airport flightpath, it was designed to withstand the direct impact of a crashing jumbo jet.

That apparently ordinary chainlink fencing would stop an assault by a speeding car; the vehicle would simply bounce straight back off it. Should some more powerful intruders, such as terrorists driving a tank, manage to penetrate the outer defenses, they would be in for a shock. The neatly manicured lawns cover deep, concrete-lined trenches into which the trespassers would plunge.

What extraordinary secrets could demand such a high level of costly and intricate defenses? Nuclear missiles or the designs for a new Stealth bomber?

The surprising answer is something far less warlike and, in many ways, considerably more valuable – detailed information on the spending habits of millions of American Express cardholders from around the world.

This is the Amex Decision Sciences Center, worldwide computer HQ for the American Express organization and the place in which data on every one of its members is stored. The building's mainframe computers know just about everything there is to know about those members: where they most like to shop, what and when they most frequently purchase, the destinations to which they travel on business or pleasure and their preferred means of transport, the restaurants they patronise, and even the economic conditions of their home countries.

By making use of this detailed personal information, American Express is able to make its members offers they find hard to refuse. Precisely targeted mailings are sent to groups of carefully selected card owners, encouraging them to invest some scarce time and attention by ensuring that each precisely corresponds to their individual interests. 'This moves us closer to true micro marketing,' notes Daniel Miller, of University College, London. 'Some offers have gone to as few as twenty people.'

This sophisticated approach to identifying the needs of New Consumers, via an analysis of what I call their tastespace, is light years away from the broadbrush techniques of segmentation; techniques that have, for decades, guided market researchers in their efforts to discover which consumers are most likely to be interested in a particular product or service. Before discussing the power and potential of tastespace, especially when marketing to the New Consumers, let us briefly review this traditional and still widely used method of determining what people might like to buy.

Why segmentation fails

It seemed like such a good idea at the time: connect televisions to the internet and achieve instant access to millions of couch potatoes eager to discover what the World Wide Web is all about, but who are baffled by computer technology. After an estimated advertising spend of $50 million had netted only 50,000 subscribers, WebTV and partners Sony and Philips Electronics admitted defeat and returned to the drawing board.

The problem was that couch potatoes simply wanted to be entertained, while internet enthusiasts were perfectly content to surf the web on PC-sized screens.

'WebTV's marketing myopia isn't unique,' comments *Business Week* journalist Paul Judge.[1] He points out that in the $280 million high-tech consumer market, companies selling products ranging from internet access through to cellular telephones, computers and software often have surprising blind spots when it comes to knowing exactly who their customers really are.

'The traditional approach pretty much always falls back on the ancient taxonomy of early adopters and followers, and that's not enough,' agrees Peter M. Winter, president of Cox Communications Inc.'s interactive media unit.

The reality of New Consumers is that they largely defy categorization – which is why segmentation, that foundation stone of market research for more than 70 years, so often fails when applied to them.

Segmentation is a deconstructive procedure that involves placing consumers in various pigeonholes bearing such labels as age, social class, frequency of product use, income and so forth. But in making general assumptions about their spending patterns and behavior, the technique can easily overlook subtle and unexpected variations. As marketing specialist Mark Sherrington puts it:

Many marketers tend to think that consumer segmentation is the best, even the only way, to segment a market. This is wrong. Segmentation is essentially about understanding how the market works and how choices get made.[2]

Sherrington's views find strong support in a recent study by consumer specialists Rachel Kennedy and Andrew Ehrenberg. They conducted an analysis of the segmentation profiles of brands in 42 UK industries. These included information on the attitudes of consumers as well as their lifestyles, demographics and media exposures. The results were bad news for all those who still regard segmentation as being an even marginally helpful marketing tool – more than nine out of ten of the differences identified turned out to be statistically insignificant. The researchers comment:

> *Brand segmentation generally does not exist. The real marketing issue is not 'who buys?' but 'how many buy?'.*[3]

Despite these well-known difficulties, qualitative researchers and advertising planners habitually use segmentation, and the way in which consumers switch between different pigeonholes, to identify marketing opportunities and give advance warning of any significant changes in consumer behavior. The backbone of segmentation methods consists of measures of statistical differences between members of a population, such as occupation, education, sex, ethnic background, size of family, postal or zip code and so on.

Information from the US Census Bureau, for example, enables us to produce a snapshot of the 'typical' American – a married white woman aged 32.7 years who graduated from high school. She is 5ft 3in tall and weighs 144lb. Last year she spent around $375 on Christmas gifts, owes $2317 on her credit card and has not made a will. She makes 3516 calls a year on her home's two telephones but she does not have an answering machine. She is most likely to be a Democrat and a Protestant who belongs to a church but does not attend services regularly.

Michael Solomon, Human Sciences Professor of Consumer Behavior at Auburn University, believes that this type of information can help 'locate and predict the size of markets for many products, ranging from home mortgages to brooms and can openers'. As an example, he suggests that you would have trouble selling 'baby food to a single male, or an around-the-world vacation to a couple making $15,000 a year'.

But this is no longer true where New Consumers are concerned. Consider, for example, the three key demographic indicators of age, gender, and income.

Age

Could you sell a computer for use by a three-year-old child or a 65-year-old senior?

Conventional marketing wisdom based on the purchasing patterns of Old Consumers would probably say 'no'. Where New Consumers are concerned, however, the answer is that this is already happening. Futurekids, a computer teaching company with eight centers in and around London, teaches children as young as three such vital skills as wordprocessing, databases, spreadsheet use, graphics, desktop publishing and multimedia. At the other end of the age spectrum, people over 60 represent one of the US's fastest-growing groups of internet users.

Gender

A typical marketing strategy for selling cigars or make-up would probably start from the assumption that men buy the smokes and women purchase lipstick. Therefore, based on gender segmentation, one should advertise cigars in male-interest publications and eye shadow in those designed for female readers. As a gross assessment this is probably correct. Yet it ignores some small yet significant markets.

The tobacco industry estimates, for example, that women now constitute up to 5 percent of the cigar market. Morton's of Chicago steakhouses have sponsored women-only smokers, while the Consolidated Cigar Corporation, which picked up on this trend early, produces a Cleopatra Collection, with cigars tapered at both ends to make them easier to light and hold.

So far as make-up is concerned, transvestites certainly purchase it in considerable quantities, but would they ever be viewed as a market segment?

What segmentation ignores is that women buy cigars for men and men purchase make-up for women. As for single males and baby food, Michael Solomon's second example of gender-specific products, with more partners sharing the childcaring chores and more lone fathers bringing up baby, this too represents a growing market that would be ignored by conventional segmentation.

Income

Marketers who believe that income must be the one segmenting tool that will unerringly slice up the population into 'prospects' and 'no-hopers' should think again. They have just fallen prey to Old Consumer thinking. Struggling to make ends meet on a low income or living lavishly on a high one has little bearing on whether or not somebody becomes a New Consumer.

New Consumerism is about lifestyle, attitudes and personal philosophy rather than income. Easily available credit allows New Consumers with limited means to display short-term spending patterns that closely resemble those of wealthier individuals. No matter how lean their means, their aspirations and desires are constantly rising.

A family on $15,000 annually who wanted to buy Solomon's 'around-the-world vacation' could almost certainly do so thanks to low-interest credit and low ticket prices in a highly competitive airline industry.

While, as I pointed out in Chapter 1, the kind of minimalist surroundings that so attract wealthy New Consumers are far from cheap, the US has also recently witnessed the growing popularity of 'cheap is chic', with wealthy shoppers haggling hard to win discounts of just a few dollars. Clearly, what is crucial here is not a small saving, but the chance to become more involved in the transaction.

From demographics to psychographics

Aware of these problems, and conscious that demographics have no feel for either individuals or lifestyles, market researchers developed a further and, they believed, more sophisticated technique of analysis and categorization: psychographics. The term, invented by Emanuel Demby, head of American marketing company Motivation Programmers Inc., involves creating psychological profiles of consumers within groups first segmented using standard demographics. Consumers are analyzed according to their interests, lifestyles, attitudes and aspirations in order to find those who share a similar profile.

In 1973, for example, US consultancy Commercial Analysts examined 360 psychographic dimensions among 4000 people to come up with eight profiles for each sex. Women might be categorized as anything from 'self-righteous conformists' or 'family-orientated church-goers' to 'fulfilled suburban matron' or 'liberated career seeker'. Similarly, men ranged from 'inconspicuous social isolates' or 'embittered resigned workers' to 'masculine hero emulators' and 'sophisticated cosmopolitans'.

Not long afterwards the Benton & Bowles advertising agency came up with a different six psychometric profiles based on a group of 2,000 housewives. Their categories were: Outgoing Optimists; Conscientious Vigilantes; Apathetic Indifferents; Self-Indulgents; Worriers and Contented Cows!

At Stanford University, SRI International developed the the Values and Lifestyles System, VALS™, which originally segmented consumers into five 'target' groups. These include 'Belongers' (the VALS definition for the Archie Bunker types of Middle America) to 'Societally-Conscious' (VALS' name for nutritionally and environmentally aware baby boomers).

In his book *The Image Makers*, former advertising executive William Meyers claims that advertisers use such information to 'exploit the weaknesses and emotions of each of the five groups', and describes how VALS™ categories were used to target soft drinks at Belongers.

Further developments led to the creation of a new VALS2™ system, which replaced earlier categories with groups ranged in order of importance to marketers. Top of this new hierarchy are Actualizers (successful consumers with many resources), while Strugglers (preoccupied with making ends meet and with limited ability to buy anything other than basics) are at the bottom of the economic heap.

One of the most recent attempts at segmenting the high-tech consumer is Technographics, developed by technology consultants Forrester Research Inc., a company based in Cambridge, Mass., whose clients for the new system, according to press reports, include Ford, Bank of America and Visa. Technographics segments people into one of 10 categories, divided into optimists and pessimists. Among the optimists are career-oriented 'Fast Forwards', who own an average of 20 technology products per household, and 'Mouse Potatoes', who use online services for entertainment and invest heavily in the latest gadgetry. Among pessimists, one finds 'Hand-Shakers', older consumers who never touch computers, and 'Traditionalists', users of technology, who are reluctant to spend on upgrades and add-ons.

The process of slotting consumers into boxes, known as taxonomies, is a major preoccupation – and source of income – for market researchers who appear to divide their time between creating more taxonomies, inventing catchy titles for them and disparaging those of other researchers. There is even one system that claims to predict spending patterns by star signs!

As a leading article in the trade journal *Admap* pointed out:

> *Most such pigeonholes are arbitrary, as often interrupting a continuum in, say, status or behaviour as marking off a real watershed between inherently dissimilar groups.*[4]

The death of segmentation

As I recounted in Chapter 2, between them, Shirley Polykoff ('Does she or doesn't she?') and Ilon Specht ('Because I'm worth it!') helped perfect a new advertising genre. In a dramatic move away from segmentation and psychographics, they promoted the idea of trying to understand the psychological relationship between individual consumers and what they choose to consume.

The creators of this radical approach were not those young copywriters, but a group of émigré European social scientists, among whom the most influential was Herta Herzog. A Viennese-trained psychoanalyst who had fled the Nazi holocaust, Herta quickly found work in the research department of Jack Tinker and Partners, an agency based in New York's Madison Avenue, the heartland of US advertising.

What marked this small agency out from the others was its development and use of motivational research, an approach whose methodology was based on the dynamic therapeutic psychology of Sigmund Freud. Herta had been one of the first to realize that the techniques that Freud had used to tease repressed memories and desires from his patients' subconscious could equally well be employed to discover what caused consumers to choose one product over another or prefer one advertising message to the next. She and her colleagues applied standard therapeutic techniques, such as hypnosis, role playing and the interpretation of Rorschach inkblots, to try to help them divine the secrets of selling.

In her approach, with its emphasis on consumers as individuals rather than members of carefully segmented groups, Herta Herzog anticipated by more than half a century a process that only today, thanks to computer technology, has become a practical possibility. That is the identification of the individual likes and dislikes, personal preferences and purchases of single consumers. The process by which this is done, known as tastespace analysis, looks set to hammer the final nail into the coffin of segmentation.

The mass market is disintegrating, splitting into smaller and smaller niches (some of which may comprise a single consumer), within which individual buying habits can be as unique and personal as fingerprints. By attempting to chop so disparate a population as New Consumers into chunks that somehow seem to go together, segmentation runs the risk of producing one-dimensional thinking about a highly multi-dimensional phenomenon.

Whenever manufacturers or marketers make it a rule to target what they view as a homogeneous market, they are increasingly likely to discover that their real customers are exceptions to that rule! Claims marketing expert Keith McNamara:

Segmentation as historically conducted by marketers is dead. The future of segmentation lies in the data already collected in organizations' computer systems. The historic data of who buys individual products is the key to creating models that predict future behavior.[5]

79

What he is talking about is a means for identifying not mass markets but individual consumers by gathering and analyzing sufficient data on their patterns of consumption and lifestyles to identify something as unique and as personal as their fingerprint – their tastespace.

The Ultimate Mall

Imagine the ultimate shopping mall, in which you could find every single product or service that has ever or could ever be devised by the human mind. Along its endless aisles and on its towering shelves you could find billions of items from every country, culture and society. All the foodstuffs that can be grown, cultivated, reared or caught on the planet would find a place in this mall, as would every type of beverage, item of clothing and footwear, computer, car, truck and aircraft. All the magazines, newspapers and books ever printed, all the audio and video tapes ever produced, package holidays to anywhere on the globe, toys, jewelry, pens, clocks, chocolates and sweets, insurance policies and pension schemes, lottery tickets and dishwashers, all located under one roof.

In short, the ultimate mall would stock the sum total of human creativity and productivity, past, present and future.

This mall is not, however, laid out in a conventional manner by product lines or categories, with all the tins of baked beans down one shelf and all the digital watches on another. Instead, it is organized around the groups of products that one individual consumer has purchased in the past and seems likely to buy in the future.

If, for example, his or her tastes in music, food and clothes include country and western, T-bone steaks and cowboy boots, then these items would be located close one another in that individual's personal tastespace. Another consumer's tastespace might have fine wines, lobster bisque and traditional jazz in close proximity.

When browsing through this ultimate mall, it makes sense for consumers to stay close to their personal tastespace, since this will be most likely to contain all the products and services that they are ever likely to need. By straying too far they risk having to squander scarce time and attention on items that have little or no appeal to them.

While browsing the ultimate mall you encounter other consumers who, because they share many aspects of your tastespace, may be viewed as kindred spirits. On other occasions you might recoil in dismay when something you had always considered uniquely your own – a remote holiday destination, a favorite restaurant or an obscure piece of music – is suddenly 'discovered' by a great many other consumers. I remember my own dismay when Puccini's aria 'Nessun Dorma' from *Turandot*, which I had long treasured, was adopted as the 1990 World Cup anthem and stayed at number two in the singles charts for several weeks. Its sudden mass popularity somehow robbed it of that special feeling that I had long held for the piece.

Consumers would benefit hugely from such a mall because the task of tracking down exactly what they wanted would be made so much easier. At the same time, they would discover new goods and services of genuine interest to them, items that previously they might only have come across by chance. For vendors, the mall would encourage a higher rate of spending as well as saving them time and money making irrelevant offers. In the ultimate mall sales would always achieve their maximum potential.

While such a mall can never become a physical entity it can, and as my American Express example shows to some extent already does, exist in cyberspace, the virtual world of computer systems.

Data mining

Cyberspace is an imaginary realm containing all our computer data, that has invented – some might say discovered – by William Gibson in his novel *Neuromancer*. He defined cyberspace as:

> *A ... graphical representation of data abstracted from the banks of every computer ... unthinkable complexity.*

The chief similarity between cyberspace and tastespace is that while neither has any objective existence, both are able to exert a profound influence over our understanding of the real world. Both are what scientists call emergent patterns, resulting not from a single cause but from the innumerable interactions of many. While the vast number of these inter-actions makes it impossible for the brain alone to make much sense of them, the enormity of the task poses no such problems for computers. By means of a technique called data mining, huge quantities of infor-mation can be analyzed, abstracting personal preferences, identifying individual choices and creating tastespace charts for every single consumer.

One major source of raw material suitable for data mining is the bio-graphical and purchasing information derived from the loyalty cards issued by retailers. These usually contain not only personal information about the owner but a record of everything they have purchased through the tills of a particular store, as well as the time, day and date on which those items were bought, providing a multidimensional view.

'It's every single one of them: even if you have a customer base of 15m, you can drill right down to an individual client,' says Mark Smith, sales and marketing director of Edinburgh-based Quadstone. His com-pany's business is developing software capable of analyzing millions of items of information from thousands of sources in order to identify the tastespace of specific consumers. Worldwide, such data mining is now worth up to £6 billion ($10 billion) annually.

> *The business people in some of these big companies have always known there are these rooms full of tapes and discs with all this data – but they've just not been able to put their hands on it or use it. They knew how many things they were selling, but they didn't really know which customer was buying what. We've allowed them to say that customer A, B or C is buying X, Y and Z.*[6]

The advantage of this approach over segmentation is twofold. First, it is a great deal faster. Data mining information from electronic point of sale (EPOS) tills in retail premises, for example, can yield relevant pat-terns of personal details and consumption preferences, and do so overnight. Second, since this approach is a bottom-up rather than top-down process, no consumer need be excluded. As a result, unexpected patterns that might have been overlooked in segmentation become immediately apparent.

Another way in which data mining can be used is to identify clusters of products that are frequently purchased together. It might be found, for instance, that consumers who buy *Hello* magazine are also likely to purchase low-fat yoghurt and diet Coke. Such an analysis would show retailers that these three items are closely associated in the tastespace of those particular consumers. Armed with this information, they would then work out what other products are most likely to be of interest and make offers based on those preferences.

Taste webs

There also exists the possibility of creating networks between consumers through which information about purchasing preferences can be exchanged, via the internet and other technologies, with any number of other interested individuals. There are several ways in which this type of network, which I call a taste web, can arise.

Taste web one: New Consumer to vendor

Consumers are obviously in the best position to provide vendors with information about their purchasing history. Collecting tastespace information allows suppliers to target their most valuable customers with the products and services most suited to their individual needs, as well as identifying opportunities for new products or services, while improving consumer satisfaction and retention. In return for providing such information, however, consumers normally expect some sort of inducement. Widely used rewards have included discounts via loyalty cards, incentive gifts for recommending the product or service to friends, or a free trial offer. While these methods have proved effective in the past, and to some extent remain so, there is evidence of growing resistance among New Consumers in particular to providing this kind of information. John Hagel and Jeffrey Rayport comment:

> *It is no secret that consumers are becoming increasingly edgy about the amount and depth of information businesses collect about them. More specifically, people are starting to realize that the information they have divulged so freely through their daily commercial transactions, financial arrangements, and survey responses has value and that they get very little in exchange for that value.*[7]

As power shifts more and more strongly to New Consumers and away from companies, Hagel and Rayport believe that organizations that they term infomediaries will be set up. These will serve as agents, brokers and custodians of personal information, which they will then market to companies on behalf of their clients, making them money while helping safeguard individual privacy.

Taste web two: Vendor to New Consumer

The vendor can provide consumers with information about a wide range of products and services, via mail or fax, over the phone and through the internet. The more carefully targeted this information – and tastespace analysis allows, as I have explained, for very precise targeting indeed – the greater the likelihood that time-poor New Consumers will attend to it.

Permission Marketing author Seth Godin appropriately used this 'giving to get' approach to marketing his own book, making the first few chapters freely available on the web to anyone who wanted to download it. 'I hope you'll be intrigued enough by this sample to go ahead and buy yourself a copy!' he explained.

Taste web three: New Consumer to New Consumer (direct)

New Consumers are increasingly banding together, forming interest groups to share their passions for anything from vintage motor cars and stamp collecting to television programs. There are, for example, websites for the 1960s television comedy *Bewitched* as well as a 1980s science fiction cyberpunk classic, *Max Headroom*. These sites exchange or sell memorabilia, discuss matters of mutual interest, and complain bitterly about any corporation that offends their delicate sensibilities. Cool hunters and mavens, whose roles we describe in Chapter 5, also provide consumer-to-consumer advice, guidance and suggestions.

Taste web four: New Consumer to New Consumer (via the seller)

Vendors can encourage loyalty by acting as channels for the flow of information between New Consumers. On the internet retailers sometimes encourage purchasers to post remarks, suggestions and criticisms about the product or service. These comments offer potential consumers useful feedback, while encouraging them to visit the site. Amazon.com, for example, publishes many reviews of its books – written for the most part by readers, whether satisfied and praising or sometimes dissatisfied and griping.

Exploiting Tastespace

While taste webs offer new avenues for exchanging the information obtained through an analysis of tastespace, the most significant benefits come from exploiting it. This may be in one of three main ways. First, it can be for micro marketing high-price, high-margin products to carefully targeted consumers who, as in the case of American Express, may number only a dozen or so.

The second use is for identifying groups of like-minded consumers whose spending history strongly suggests they could be interested in the product or service. One company that has developed the technology needed to achieve this powerful marketing technique is Capital One, which with 18 million customers and account growth running at 40 percent is one of the fastest-expanding credit-card companies in the US.

Capital One is able to predict the nature of incoming calls before they are even made, and direct the caller to an agent most likely to know the answers. Those customers who simply want to check their balance are directed to a computer, while any whose queries are complex are routed to an employee – and all this before the phone has even rung. The secret lies in a careful analysis of calling patterns, which allows up to 70 percent of all customers' needs to be correctly predicted, so saving the company time and providing a more efficient service. 'We can answer your question before you ask it,' says Capital One's chief information officer Jim Donehey. 'That's the genius of the system.'[8]

But as Capital One's co-chief, British expatriate and a former social worker Nigel Morris, cheerfully concedes, there is even more genius in the system than might at first be apparent. That lies in the opportunities for cross-selling to people whose tastespace is already known when they call into the company. A computer capable of predicting a caller's most likely question can, after all, also anticipate their interest in virtually any other type of service or product, from mortgages to cell phones. 'A cell phone,' Morris points out, 'is just a credit card with an antenna.'[9]

The third use of tastespace analysis is for pre-selling a product, before it has even been created. This, suggests Seth Godin, may be the real aim and ambition of Amazon.com, which, he comments, is in big trouble if it really sees its future as being a bookseller. Its smaller scale of purchase means it is paying more for its books than Barnes & Noble, and a growing number of online booksellers will certainly be able to compete on price. 'So why is Amazon so busy building its customer base, losing money on each customer and trying to make it up in volume?' he pertinently demands. His answer is that payday will arrive when Amazon stops selling books and starts publishing.

If, for example, an analysis of its customers' tastespace showed that a million were interested in mystery novels by a particular author, it could e-mail all those readers and ask whether they would like to purchase the next mystery novel by that author, which would only be available through Amazon. If a third of those readers agreed and pre-ordered the book, Seth suggests, Amazon could contact the author, offer him or her a million dollars to write it and still make a profit of millions itself. And that would be on just one book. Repeat the same exercise a hundred or a thousand times and you have not only created the world's most financially successful publisher, but reduced the current publishing production line to just two elements, the writer and Amazon.

Recommendation engines

Once tastespace has begun to be mapped it can be used to everyone's advantage. This starts at the basic level of 'customers who bought product A, B and C also bought products X, Y and Z'. The discovery of a correlation between these products can then be passed on to the consumer.

In another approach to creating tastespace for books, www.alexlit.com allows readers to view lists of books and rate the extent to which they enjoyed those they have read. After a particular person has rated around 40, the site is able to provide a list of books they have not read but would probably enjoy. The greater the number visiting the site, the more accurately the recommendations will reflect an individual's tastespace. A similar service is offered by the website 'If you like...' (www.ifyoulike.com), which offers consumers recommendations across a range of products including films, music and books.

Taste-satisfying machinery

New Consumers' attraction to bespoke purchases has led to a demand for products they can use to create things for themselves, such as music, graphics, animations and professionally edited home videos. This trend looks set to accelerate as more and more low-cost digital cameras, camcorders, audio recorders and editing software reach the marketplace. Fashion houses may soon offer websites on which one can design, with professional help, an entirely original wardrobe that will then be made up in their workshops. Car manufacturers may provide the means for drivers to design their own specifications on a standard model, testing out different color schemes and interior layouts. Korean Daewoo Corporation offered a similar service in its showrooms.

When Intuition Replaces Computer Power

While computers are essential for handling the vast amounts of data obtained through loyalty cards and similar information-gathering methods, they are seldom appropriate or practical for much smaller companies. The cost of the equipment and processing aside, there will always be a large number of businesses which, because of their size or limited a range of products, find it impractical to search for spending patterns among their consumers.

The alternative to using computers to access tastespace is human intuition, something successful businesspeople have been employing for generations, based on developing an insight into the way their customers' minds work – sometimes called a feeling for the marketplace. Such insights may come about as result of having spent many years working in a particular field or through an empathy derived from a deep and genuine interest in the product(s) or service(s) being sold as well as in those to whom you are making the sale.

One man with an intuitive feeling for what New Consumers want to buy is Richard Branson. As he explains in his autobiography *Losing My Virginity*: 'I rely far more on gut instinct than researching huge amounts of statistics.' Time and again, from records to airline seats and vodka to financial services, that instinct has proved a more accurate judge of market trends than any amount of statistical analysis.

Most of us probably know of at least one enthusiastic specialist who lives and breathes whatever it is he or she sells. In the future, such personally involved suppliers will not only be in a strong position to fight back against impersonal, and sometimes product-ignorant, salespeople in vast companies and superstores, but will also gain a positive advantage. Their personal passion and wealth of knowledge will prove massively attractive to New Consumers in search of authenticity of service, which comes from individual attention and expert knowledge.

The other occasion when intuition may offer a surer guide than computer analysis is in marketing a new product. This is because the ways in which New Consumers especially will respond to something different may not always be apparent from their current purchases. Only once the product or service has been introduced and they have had a chance to sample it can their level of interest be judged.

Summary

◆ The surest way to identify products and services of greatest appeal to New Consumers is not through traditional segmentation but by means of tastespace analysis.

◆ The top-down approach of segmentation inevitably ignores or fails to identify developing niche markets, and leads companies to reject innovative niche products and services that have potential wider appeal.

◆ Segmentation defines who the likely customers of a product are — mainly for the benefit of marketers. But traditional market segmentation does not allow us to understand the New Consumer fully. This is because it makes assumptions about consumers' behavior that often ignore subtle or unexpected patterns of purchasing.

◆ Unlike segmentation, tastespace makes no assumptions about who will buy a product and therefore does not artificially limit the target market.

◆ Tastespace represents the ultimate shopping mall where everything you ever want to buy is available and collected together.

◆ By analysing tastespace it is possible to target commercial messages, as well as products and services themselves, to those groups of New Consumers most likely to show a genuine interest in learning about them.

◆ Many highly successful entrepreneurs use market knowledge and intuition rather than computers to analyze consumer tastespace, and this is often the only route open to smaller organizations or those striving to bring original products and services to the market.

5

Why Buzz Beats Hype:
Cool Hunters, Mavens and the
New Consumers

The trick is not just to be able to tell who is different but to be able to tell when that difference represents something truly cool. It's a gut thing. You have to somehow know.

Malcolm Gladwell, 'The Coolhunt'

Mark Wentworth is a cool hunter. At the age of 31, this former make-up artist has become a Sherlock Holmes of color, his opinions and predictions in constant demand by companies wanting to know what colours are sufficiently 'cool' to catch the eye of a New Consumer.

Tall, blond and boyish, Mark was wearing black when we met at a restaurant in the heart of London's Soho. 'Black helps make people less visible,' he explains, 'it allows you blend with the background.'

Blending with the background is important to cool hunters, who need to see without being seen and observe without themselves becoming the objects of observation by others. Not that black is cool any longer. 'Black is an eighties shade,' says Mark, 'black and brushed aluminium reflected the combination of insecurities and technical inno-vation that was the hallmark of that era.'

Gray, Mark informed his corporate clients, was set to become the new black of the late 1990s, and so it came to pass. That's the skill of being a cool hunter – knowing what will be and what will never be in the world of trends, providing manufacturers of everything from paint to clothing accessories with early warning about what colors and styles are set to become fashionable when they are still only being recognized and appreciated by small groups of early innovators.

'The gay community is a great place to spot the start of a trend,' com-ments Mark, 'not just for color but for music, fashion and interior design. So much that will be cool for straights starts out by being cool for gays.'

'I predicted that the start of the millennium would see a return to the early decades of the twentieth century,' he continues. 'Edwardian elegance in clothes, décor, accessories and drapes will come into its own. There will be a certain decadence in designs, with flavors of Oscar Wilde and Aubrey Beardsley. Vibrant colors will be in vogue, with indigo becoming the coolest of cool colors.'

Later we visit West End stores where he points out early indications of his predictions becoming reality. In upmarket retailer Liberty, there are jackets in vibrant, outrageous colors and designs, tasseled Edwardian smoking caps and handbags with such colorful and elabo-rate beadwork they could be mistaken for costume props from *Titanic*.

'Cool?' I inquire. Mark shakes his head.

'Not cool,' he corrects, 'supercool.'

In the US, Mark's equivalent is cool hunter DeeDee Gordon, who works for an advertising agency and publishes the quarterly *L Report* for which companies pay around $20,000 a year.

DeeDee explained to Malcolm Gladwell, a writer for *New Yorker* magazine, that the secret of being a successful cool hunter is first to find cool people:

> *Since cool things are always changing, you can't look for them, because the very fact they are cool means you have no idea what to look for ... Cool people, on the other hand, are a constant.*[1]

But tracking down cool people is a far from easy task. As Piney Kahn, who works for DeeDee, explains, there are lots of people who look as though they could be cool but turn out not to be: 'You've got these kids who dress ultra funky and have their own style. Then you realize they're just running after their friends.'

Mark's territory includes clubs, pubs, street markets and fashion shows; not the big, glitzy shows that often only reflect trends already in decline, but displays of work by college students and emerging designers and artists. Mark talks endlessly to cool youngsters, white kids, black kids, Asian kids, gay kids and straight kids, not only in London, Paris and Milan but in provincial towns and cities where cool is germinating in back bedrooms, design classes and craft workshops.

Cool hunters like Mark and DeeDee have the knack of being able to find out what's new and exciting at street level and then separate them into robustly growing trends and rapidly fading fads. It is a talent you can never learn and only possess if you too happen to be truly cool. 'That's the essence of the third rule of cool,' says Malcolm Gladwell, 'you have to be one to know one.'

This is what makes cool hunters thin on the ground and greatly in demand by major companies, which seldom have any other fast and reliable means of keeping in touch with what New Consumers are most likely to buy.

Just how influential cool hunters can prove is well illustrated by the slightly bizarre tale of Hush Puppies' sudden rise from extremely uncool obscurity to fame and fortune in the supercool world of high fashion.

The Hush Puppies story

At the start of the 1990s Hush Puppies, classic brushed-suede casual shoes with lightweight crepe soles, were in trouble. Their Oxford design, known as the Duke, and their Columbia, a slip-on shoe with a golden buckle, were selling barely 65,000 pairs a year and the company, based in Rockford, Michigan, was preparing to drop the suede casual in favour of a new 'active casual' in smooth leather. Then it started picking up an unexpected buzz from Manhattan. In the Village, they were told, young people were hunting down and snapping up Hush Puppies in the resale shops and small footwear stores still stocking them. They were seeking, in the words of Hush Puppies executive Owen Baxter, the 'authenticity of being able to say, "I am wearing an original pair of Hush Puppies".' The word on the streets was that Hush Puppies were cool.

The first call to the company came from fashion designer John Bartlett, who wanted to feature them as accessories in his spring collection. Soon after that, Joel Fitzpatrick gutted the art gallery he owned next to his store in La Brea Avenue, Los Angeles, and transformed it into a Hush Puppies emporium. At the peak of the revival, Hush Puppies won the prize as the best accessory at the Council of Fashion Designers' awards dinner at the Lincoln Center. The company's president Louis Dubrow collected it wearing custom-made black patent leather Hush Puppies. Malcolm Gladwell reported:

> *It was a strange moment. There was the president of Hush Puppies company … sharing a stage with Calvin Klein and Donna Karan and Isaac Mizrahi – and all because some kids in the East Village began combing through thrift shops for old Dukes. Fashion was at the mercy of those kids.*[2]

The Hush Puppies story provides two valuable lessons for all marketers wanting to sell products or services to New Consumers.

First, it illustrates the extraordinary power of buzz. The word started to get around that Hush Puppies gave you the coolest feet on the street and soon a trickle of demand was causing them to disappear from dusty shelves. Fashion designer and Isaac Mizrahi started wearing them for his personal use. The trickle turned into a stream and soon after into a torrent of demand – within two years 600,000 people were buying Hush Puppies. It was a triumph that no amount of costly hype could hope to emulate. I shall be discussing the differences between buzz and hype later in the chapter.

The second lesson is the power of cool hunters to spot a trend in the making, so accelerating its progress through their personal and professional endorsement.

Mavens – the Power Behind Sales Success

While cool hunters mostly act as consultants to big business, another well-informed and highly influential group of consumers known as mavens operate at a far more local and grassroots level. Although mavens are occasionally paid by companies to promote their products or services, the great majority are unpaid enthusiasts, individuals who delight in learning about some particular aspect of consuming, such as food and drink, clothes or cars, and then passing on their expertise – free of charge – to friends, colleagues and, indeed, anyone who seeks them out and asks for help.

Because mavens are regarded as both knowledgeable and objective, their views are usually taken very seriously and their advice is often acted on, especially by time-scarce New Consumers. As a result, the views of just a few thousand mavens have the power to influence the purchasing patterns of millions of shoppers, making these anonymous men and women an economic force that no producer or supplier should ever underestimate.

According to Linda Price, professor of marketing at the University of South Florida, who first came up with the term in the late 1980s, mavens are the most powerful and influential of all the New Consumers. They are the connoisseurs of consumption, possessing an almost encyclopaedic knowledge of products, prices and the best places to shop. Price explains:

Mavens initiate discussions with consumers and respond to their requests. They take you shopping. They go shopping for you, and it turns out that they are a lot more prevalent than you would expect.

The distribution of mavens does not vary by ethnic category, by income or by professional status. A working woman is just as likely as a non-working woman to be a market maven. Not surprisingly mavens are not only great guides for others, but within their area of expertise they are also far better consumers themselves, being very 'features' oriented and rarely overly impressed by promotions.

'You can reach them,' says Linda Price, 'but it's an intellectual argument.'

There are four main type of maven, each addressing a different constituency and each possessing different qualifications for the job.

Neighborhood mavens

The most prevalent, and in many ways most persuasive, of all mavens is an unpaid enthusiast who looks on most shopping as an enjoyable leisure activity. Within their self-selected area of expertise, these neighborhood mavens keep themselves well informed about the latest trends and fashions, spend a great deal of time window shopping, compare prices, check quality and track down the best deals.

The essential quality needed to become a neighborhood maven is a deep passion for shopping, coupled with an eye for quality and design, an instinct for what will develop into tomorrow's hot items, and a readiness to experiment with the latest products and designs. Not only are these mavens eager to be among the first to buy and try such items, even more importantly, they like to be *seen* to be first. And therein lies their value. They are the risk takers who will switch to a new product before the rest of the marketplace, proudly demonstrate it for their friends, and generate a buzz of excitement by discussing it with almost anyone willing to listen. Their actions are eagerly watched and their opinions sought by other consumers who want to know how good these new products are and whether they think it's worth buying them.

When enough mavens start raving about anything new in the marketplace, whether it is a film, a book, a restaurant, a piece of music or a mobile phone, sales are likely to soar.

Professional mavens

These are individuals whose job or qualifications give them genuine authority or expertise in a specific area. Into this category come a whole host of specialists, including film, book and music reviewers, restaurant

95

and theater critics, motoring correspondents, fashion and shopping editors and consumer consultants on TV and in print.

One type of professional maven, with a clearly somewhat less than objective view of the products he or she suggests, is employed by high-class stores to assist well-heeled and high-status customers locate exactly what they are seeking with only minimal expenditure of time and attention on their part. These highly experienced mavens give advice to princes and presidents on which products to buy, and will even go around the store doing the buying – although not of course the paying – on their behalf. With a minimum spend of around £50,000 per shopping trip and A List celebrity membership as the most basic requirements, such mavens are clearly only available to a tiny minority of shoppers.

Far more democratic are the *karisuma* (charisma) shop assistants, a major craze among many of Japan's fashion and luxury goods retailers as the old millennium drew to a close. *Karisuma,* who can be found in everything from clothes shops to hair salons, are young women whose images or services have come to be perceived by teenage girls as representing the pinnacles of fashion and individuality. They are employed by such retailers as Egoist, a pocket-handkerchief-sized shop selling 1970s-style dresses from the fourth floor of 109, a trendy shopping center in downtown Tokyo. In 1999, Egoist's star *karisuma* was Yoko Morimoto, a 22-year-old who wore a wig of flowing brown hair with bleached blonde highlights, five-inch platform sandals, a nose ring and long pink fingernails. Such was her popularity that magazines and television stations regularly requested interviews, while her young customers regarded her as a more potent fashion icon than any pop singer or TV actress.[3]

The power of professional mavens to make even an apparently dull product into a mass seller is illustrated by the curious story of the humble cardigan's sudden rise to fame.[4] For years, this garment had been dismissed as a frumpy relic of the 1950s. In the early 1990s it started to become fashionable again after minimalist designers, in particular Prada, introduced it into their collection. After it was worn by followers of new-wave grunge bands such as Pearl Jam and Nirvana, a trend rapidly grew so that, by the end of the century, it was virtually impossible to open a gossip magazine without finding celebrities wearing psychedelic cardigans, designed by Marc Jacobs or Matthew Williams, at award ceremonies and film premières. The cardigan achieved economic as well as social status when it was given the accolade of inclusion in the UK's Retail Price Index (RPI), the official barometer for consumer spending. Items are only included in the RPI if they sell in such numbers that the level of demand could affect general trends in expenditure.

Fanatical mavens

The internet enables fans of virtually anything and everything – from locomotives to rock groups, *Dr Who* to *Star Wars* – to share their passions over the web. Even a product as seemingly innocuous as Lego bricks has inspired more than 30 fan-produced websites and net-based news groups. The more a product embodies a distinctive philosophy or vision, such as Apple computers or *Star Trek*, the more likely New Consumers are to form fan groups around it.

The process by which devoted but nerdy fans coalesce on the internet has been rather unkindly described as 'cluster geeking', highlighting their potential to form influential consumer communities. Their main weakness as reliable mavens, however, is a certain tunnel vision that often prevents them ever accepting that the product or service they so passionately admire could ever possess even minor flaws or failings.

Celebrity mavens

The final group of mavens, although generally more influential among Old than New Consumers, can sometimes trigger a spending frenzy that involves both groups. They are able to achieve this measure of power and persuasion not through any particular knowledge or expertise, but merely because they enjoy huge and often international celebrity. Because their every comment is extensively reported by the mass media, the views of celebrity mavens frequently receives far greater prominence than it deserves.

In the US, the reading habits of Presidents can transform almost any book into an overnight bestseller. President Kennedy, a James Bond fan, famously launched Ian Fleming's early novels into orbit, as did President Reagan's admiration for Tom Clancy's first novel, *The Hunt for Red October*.

While regarded as a powerful marketing tool, when measured by the amount of buzz – at least short term – that a celebrity maven endorsement provides, we believe there are two main problems in using them to attract distrustful New Consumers. The first is that well-informed, streetwise consumers know perfectly well that in many instances the celebrity maven is being paid, probably extremely well paid, to make such an endorsement. This transforms buzz into hype, and – for reasons I will discuss in a moment – devalues it in the eyes of New Consumers. Indeed, it can rebound on the product, making genuine buzz appear equally suspect and unworthy of consideration.

The second problem is that because celebrity mavens exert their influence from the top down, their influence is less likely to survive at grassroots level.

There are, of course, exceptions. Sporting celebrity mavens promoting anything from trainers to golf clubs have a degree of authenticity about themselves and their endorsements that allow even cynical New Consumers to trust their judgments. The same applies across a wide range of celebrities who are also acknowledged experts in their own right. But when a celebrity attempts, or is encouraged, to act as a maven in an area where she or he is not perceived as having specialist knowledge, the ploy is as likely to be dismissed by a majority of New Consumers even when generally accepted by Old Consumers.

Even celebrity animals, it seems, can sometimes provide 'endorsements' that will be regarded as authentic by some consumers. While conducting studies in a supermarket not long ago, one of our researchers heard an elderly couple discussing which tea to buy. Pointing to a box of PG Tips, a brand for years associated with televisions commercials that show the tea being drunk by a family of chimpanzees, the man said to his partner: 'Let's try a packet of those. Them chimps speak very highly of them!'

The maven's three sources of power

Today we all have the potential to possess almost as much knowledge as suppliers have about goods and services, their availability, pricing, financing options, and the alternatives available from competing firms. The key caveat here is 'potential'. For while every New Consumer can in theory track down such information, they rarely have sufficient time to do so.

The result is a growing reliance among New Consumers on finding others who are ready, willing and able to ferret out the information on their behalf, and it is from this need that mavens derive their first source of power. This remains true whether they are full time, paid, professionals or enthusiastic amateurs, willing to share the fruits of their labors with friends and colleagues.

While it is easy to see how professional mavens find the time to search for and disseminate their specialist consumer knowledge – it is after all their livelihood – it may seem paradoxical that time-pressured New Consumers, for no financial or commercial return, are able and willing to do the same. The explanation is that they are so fascinated, excited and enthused by the products or services in which they become expert that such time is seen as invested rather than wasted. It is invested in enjoyment and the thrill of the chase, invested in the sense of satisfaction that comes from tracking down a bargain and getting a better price than other, less well-informed shoppers.

This kind of enthusiasm causes Cynthia Hemming, the managing director of my research consultancy and herself a respected fashion maven, to set aside time in her hectic schedule for a little 'shopping therapy' – her favorite brands are currently Max Mara, Sisley and Jil Sander. She explains:

> *There are times when I need to come right out of my work, and I find that helping friends and colleagues shop for the latest fashion a perfect way of relaxing.*

The maven's second source of power stems directly from the distrust that a majority of New Consumers feel when purchasing unfamiliar products or services from suppliers they do not know. Mindful of the potential for making bad and possibly costly decisions, they seek a specialist to guide them through alien territory. They recognize that in addition to possessing considerable knowledge about a particular product or service, mavens are usually aware of the tricks and stratagems that may be used on the unwary. Researcher Gregory Schmid comments:

> *The United States spent almost a century building a regulatory network to protect citizens from the complex risks of a rich, urbanized, industrialized society. Now a more sophisticated consumer, new technologies, and a much more competitive global marketplace are gradually creating an environment more self-regulating and open to consumer discretion, an environment in which it is easier to spread throughout the marketplace the risk that was formerly taken on by the government.*[5]

This is a trend that marketing consultant and futurologist Faith Popcorn has termed 'vigilante consumerism'. She says:

> *We, vigilante consumers, seek substance over style. Truth over packaging. Answers, not press releases.*[6]

The third factor placing increasing power into the hands of mavens is that the sheer abundance of products and services makes it increasingly difficult and confusing for non-experts to decide which one will best meet their specific needs.

In the US alone, for example, more than 35,000 branded goods are currently being advertised, while the average hypermarket can stock up to 40,000 different items. With choice set to expand even further over the coming years, thanks in large part to the internet, assessing every product is going to prove such an impossible challenge for the vast majority of New Consumers that they will be obliged to rely more and more on the judgments of mavens.

Cool Hunters and Mavens – the True Market Makers

While the importance of cool hunters and mavens as makers or break-ers of markets is fairly easy to understand where such faddish products as pop music, computer games, video, film and television production, fashion and fashion accessories are concerned, their significance in other areas of manufacturing may seem tenuous or even non-existent.

Do the instincts of cool hunters and the views of mavens really mat-ter to companies that, for example, make kitchen appliances, motor cars, mobile phones, computers or garden furniture?

The answer is that they matter a great deal, if not by directly influ-encing designs and features then by shaping the cultural milieu into which all products aimed at New Consumers must fit. Indeed, even those companies solely concerned with products intended for mass marketing and mass consumption to Old Consumers are to some extent affected by cool trends at street level.

Any commercial organization ignores the power of these market mak-ers at its peril. Of all the new products introduced into European and US markets in 1998, only 20 percent enjoyed any commercial success. At least in part this was due to the growing influence of cool hunters and mavens and their ability to distinguish new products with genuine bene-fits from the host of superfluous 'me-too' items, no matter how strongly the latter were promoted or how enthusiastically they were hyped.

If you can convince a maven that your product or service is worth buying then they in turn will convince other consumers – whether it be fewer than a dozen to many millions – to buy it as well.

Because of their unbiased expertise, their views acquire a high level of authenticity, which makes them especially influential with New Consumers. As a result, they offer the reassurance that the recom-mended products or services are also authentic. They spare New Consumers the need to invest scarce time or attention in a purchase, either by cutting through the plethora of choice or by actually doing the shopping on another's behalf.

The moral for manufacturers and suppliers, therefore, is that while it is important to win the confidence of New Consumers, it is even more vital to impress the mavens who serve as their representatives.

At present it could be argued that too much attention is devoted to impressing professional mavens, by offering a host of eagerly snapped up 'freebies', which may include expenses-paid holidays in exotic locations, loans or gifts of prestige products, invitations to sales conferences and exhibitions with luxury travel included and so on.

While the power of many professional mavens to spread their views widely through direct access to the media is not in doubt, consideration should also be given to winning over neighborhood mavens, those enthusiastic and well-informed amateurs who may be the relative, friend, neighbor or colleague of a New Consumer. With the web now becoming an even more important, informative and influential source of advice and guidance for many New Consumers than newspapers, magazines or TV, the influence of professional mavens is less powerful and persuasive than it once was.

Neighborhood mavens can also promote products through grass-roots exchanges that can, in some cases, spread with astonishing speed through whole communities and, via the internet, across national frontiers. Such community-based exchanges are trusted to a far greater extent and given much greater credence than suggestions and advice handed down from on high. They are a thousand times more influential than paid-for advertising or endorsement by celebrity mavens. This is the difference between hype and buzz.

Buzz vs Hype

The success of the movie *The Blair Witch Project* offers a perfect example of the power of word-of-mouth buzz to outpace even the most expensive hype when generating excitement among New Consumers.

After its first showing, at a midnight screening on the first day of the 1999 Sundance Film Festival in Florida, the movie's prospects seemed far from bright. Buyers received the film politely rather than rapturously and it was clear that finding a distributor might be far from easy. The makers were delighted, therefore, when a small New York-based company called Artisan Entertainment made a bid. It was the only one they had. To the derision of other distributors, Artisan paid $1 million for the distribution rights. 'The scariest thing about *The Blair Witch Project* is that anyone would pay $1 million for it,' sneered a competitor.[7]

But he reckoned without the power of buzz and the internet. Co-writer and director Eduardo Sanchez set up a Blair Witch website, Blairwitch.com, that supposedly traces the story back to the eighteenth century and the mysterious disappearance of a group of village children. The website is designed in such a way that to find their way around it, visitors had to become involved in the story. The style is quasi-academic, with unemotional descriptions of such horrors as disembowelment. By the time the movie was released a trickle of visitors had turned into a flood, with the Blair Scare being actively discussed in internet chat rooms by influential US New Consumers.

What works for films works equally well for books. Take Harry Potter, an 11-year-old wizard created in 1997 by British author J.K. Rowling. Since Harry's first appearance more than 5 million copies of Rowling's books have been sold worldwide, 3 million of them in the United States, and almost all this enormous success has been achieved through grassroots buzz rather than marketing hype. To build an interest in the US, for example, her American publishers Scholastic started a word-of-mouth campaign months before the first book appeared, sending copies to influential mavens including critics, librarians and, perhaps most importantly of all, children. In the word's of Scholastic's marketing manager Jennifer Pasamen, this was 'our own universe of big mouths'.[8] Such was the buzz that Harry Potter generated that the $18 hardcover copies flew from the shelves, while impatient US Potterphiles ordered early copies of Rowling's next book via Amazon.co.uk. Despite criticism from some church groups that Rowling is promoting the black arts, US interest has been so great that Amazon.co.uk will not ship more than one copy per order of any Harry Potter book to the US, even the first one.

Contrast this with the abject failure of hype to transform the fortunes of the movie *Godzilla* which, despite a promotional spend in excess of $200 million, returned gross US box office receipts of only $136 million.

Informed, independent-minded and individualistic New Consumers can usually spot hyperbole at a thousand paces and are no longer impressed or persuaded by chrome-plated gimmickry. Gary Hamel and Jeff Sampler point out:

> *As advertisers have pegged the hype-o-meter at 100, consumers have developed their b.s. detectors. No wonder more and more consumers are looking to get their information from someone who is unbiased.*[9]

It is not only consumers who are tending to place a high value on the opinions of other consumers. Many in the entertainment and publishing industry are now paying a great deal of attention to views expressed over the internet. It was internet buzz, rather than agent's hype, that brought a £675,000, nine-book publishing deal to novice author Steven Erikson, a communications executive with Toyota cars.

When American-born Steven's first novel, *Gardens of the Moon*, was published by Bantam in the Spring of 1999, the book attracted only a small advance and modest sales. But those who did read it became so excited by his serious, upmarket fantasy tale that they quickly spread the news via the internet. Such was their enthusiasm – some describing Erikson as 'the new face of everything' – that his agent, Patrick Walsh, was able to persuade Transworld to make him every author's dream offer. Walsh comments:

> *This shows that the internet is now far more powerful than reviewers. What kicked in everyone's attention was that fans were promoting Steven among themselves.*[10]

Buzz is the natural, authentic version of hype. It is the infectious chatter that spreads from consumer to consumer about something of genuine interest to them. The subject of the buzz could be a product, service, place, person, TV show or even an idea. Buzz is created and spread among consumers at street level. In contrast hype, generated at the corporate level, is targeted *at* consumers. Buzz, says writer Nancy Austin, is the 'CNN of the street'.

Buzz usually tells the truth – be it good or bad – about a product and so rates high on credibility. Because hype is always intended to promote it is viewed with increasing cynicism and distrust by New Consumers, especially if they have had personal experience of a product or service that failed to live up to the hype.

Log onto smartgirl.com and you can discover exactly what teenage girls and young women have to say about almost every aspect of popular consumer culture, from cosmetics to movies and magazines to celebrities. According to a recent listing, Will Smith is on the way up, along with butterfly hairclips and the preppy look, while Leonardo Di Caprio is on the way down in the company of Tommy Hilfiger. Some of the product reviews are brutal enough to make a brand manager's hair turn grey overnight. 'Don't unless you really feel like wasting your money on a product that will ruin your hair,' warns 16-year-old Aoife of a popular shampoo, while another shampoo receives this blunt thumbs-down from 17-year-old Julia: 'If you want a gift for your worst enemy, buy this crap.'

Buzz is fast overtaking hype in terms of persuasiveness as New Consumers become better informed and increasingly connected to sources of expertise. While hype takes time, effort and expense to circulate, buzz can move like wildfire through a community. The table below shows some of the main differences between these two forms of promotion.

	Buzz	**Hype**
Style	Democratic	Autocratic
Content	More likely to be regarded as truthful	More likely to be regarded as devious
Typical media	Conversations, websites, e-mail	Press, advertising
Examples	Rumors, gossip	Press releases
New Consumers' reaction	Trust	Distrust

To New Consumers street buzz, whether spread by word of mouth or via the internet, is far more influential than any amount of hype. Once persuaded by buzz, however, both New and Old Consumers become far more receptive to hype.

This powerful marketing combination of positive buzz followed up by advertising hype is well illustrated by US petfood company Iams Co., based in Dayton, Ohio. At the time it started to create a buzz about its more nourishing food, the majority of America's 57 million dog and 70 million cat owners were content to pick up a bag of Dog Chow or 9-Lives from the supermarket shelves. Rather than tackle entrenched consumer habits head on, Iams targeted its campaign, based on the importance of sound nutrition to a pet's health, at such professional mavens as vets, breeders and kennel owners, whose advice would be trusted. Iams approached the task of changing the eating habits of the nation's pets with almost evangelical zeal, CEO Clay Mathilde likening the task to that of 'missionaries, out there saving the world's dogs and cats'.

Once the buzz began, owners concerned for the wellbeing of their pets quickly took notice, transforming Iams into one of the fastest-moving companies in the $2 billion speciality petfood market and increasing sales from $16 million to more than $500 million.

How New Ideas Are Adopted – Buzz and Diffusion

Diffusion is the process by which new ideas and innovations spread throughout a community.

One of the earliest and most famous studies of diffusion involved not streetsmart Manhattan kids and their choice of footwear, but farmers in Greene County, Iowa, and the rate at which they plated new hybrid corn seeds, far superior to the traditionally planted crop. In 1928, when the seeds were introduced, researchers Bruce Ryan and Neal Gross decided to study how quickly the hybrid was taken up by farmers spread across the county. Five years after it was first introduced, only a few had switched to the hybrid and by 1934 the number had still only risen to 16. In 1935, 21 more followed their example and by 1937 there were

61, but it took another four years before all 259 had adopted the new seed.

The few adventurous farmers who started using the hybrid at the start of the 1930s were termed innovators. The slightly larger group who had switched by 1935 were early adopters, careful, thoughtful folk rather than risk-taking innovators. They were the kind of people who liked to wait and see what happened before deciding which way to jump. Those who came after them were known as the early majority, who will not take on anything new until early adopters, whose views they respect, have shown it to be safe. Only once a new idea has firmly taken root do the remaining categories of late adopters and finally laggards make the change.

Diffusion is now a well-established marketing principle, with the associated terms being applied to the speed with which consumers take up new products or services. My preferred term for innovators is alpha consumers, to emphasize that this risk-taking, curiosity-satisfying, adventurous group is at the forefront when it comes to picking up on new ideas and fresh trends.

Buzz is created when cool hunters (alpha consumers) pick up on the latest fashion and start generating interest in the product or service. This is then amplified through the interest of mavens (early adopters), who persuade a large number of New Consumers (early majority) to follow their lead and start spreading the buzz further afield.

From there it moves to the late majority (a mixture of New and Old Consumers) and finally to laggards (entirely comprised of Old Consumers), by which time the trend has largely been supplanted by the latest buzz.

Cool Hunters, Mavens and the Cycle of Innovation

The rate at which head-turning innovations are transformed into so-what commodities grows ever faster with each year that passes. When the first domestic telephones appeared on the market, around the mid-1870s, those wealthy enough to afford a private line ensured that at least one phone was placed in the hallway. This choice of location was made not on the basis of convenience – it was usually the least comfortable and draughtiest place to make or take a phone call – but for the purposes of prestige. There was little point in being sufficiently affluent to possess a telephone if casual callers never got to see it. It took the best part of half a century for the telephone to become truly public property and lose any attributes of status.

Similarly, when the first televisions began to appear in UK homes, during the late 1940s, they too were luxury items that made their owners the talk of the neighborhood. By 1949 only 126,567 sets had been licensed, and those wealthy enough to possess one of the black-and-white sets, with their poor picture quality based on 425 lines, would be singled out for attention by neighbors eager to get invited for an evening's 'viewing'. In this case the cycle of innovation was far shorter. In 1943 the US, for instance, there were 10,000 owners served by six television stations across the nation, a figure limited by wartime restrictions. By 1949, with these removed, there were one million set owners, with ten million sets being viewed just three years later. By the start of the 1960s that number had risen to 50 million.

The same cycle of innovation applied to pocket calculators, personal computers, digital watches, fax machines and mobile phones, only in each case the once leisurely cycle of innovation spun them from status symbol to unexciting commodity in months rather than years. Soon it may be only a matter of weeks before the market value of once-prized possessions has been driven down to the point where they are either given away free or sold at knockdown prices.

As the cycle of innovation spins ever faster, the window of opportunity for companies to make money from the latest developments – or at least to avoid losing business to speedier competitors – becomes ever narrower, while the need for cool hunters and mavens will become ever more urgent.

Success over the next decade for an increasing number of product and service providers will crucially depend, therefore, on latching on to new trends while they still possess that aura of authenticity so sought after by New Consumers, then transforming them into commodities as rapidly as possible, and starting to pick up on and promote the next innovation almost before the dust has settled on the first.

One of the most obvious, and essential, characteristics of both cool hunters and mavens is their high degree of involvement in the marketplace. Cool hunters, especially, can exert a direct and profound impact on the products that make it from design department to consumer outlets. Mavens, although their involvement is usually less immediate, often have their ideas and suggestions taken sufficiently seriously by manufacturers and service providers to change the look, feel or marketing of new products.

Involvement is also an important issue for those New Consumers who make up the early and late majorities. By encouraging involvement, manufacturers can automatically engage their attention and persuade them to invest some scarce time in examining their product or service. They are also more likely to build trust and satisfaction. After all, if you have had a hand in the creation of a product or service it is only natural to feel some kind of emotional attachment, and to regard it as more authentic than one in which you have had no role to play. Clearly, therefore, the greater the consumer involvement companies can provide for and encourage, the better it will be for their profitability.

Identifying Cool Hunters and Mavens

Companies interested in promoting their products or services by means of grassroots buzz as well as, or in addition to, traditional marketing hype, should develop ways of reaching cool hunters and neighborhood mavens, rather than focusing all their efforts on those in the celebrity or professional categories.

One method for identifying them will, in time, be by analysing their tastespace, as discussed in the previous chapter. They could be identified from their purchasing patterns, which would include many new and innovative products in the case of cool hunters and a large number of 'value for money' items in the case of mavens. Unfortunately, until EPOS data or information from smart loyalty cards becomes far more comprehensively available, accurate identification is unlikely to be sufficiently reliable to have much commercial value.

The second method of making contact is via the internet, for example by contacting consumers who, like some of the readers on Amazon.com, show sufficient interest in the products being sold to write unpaid reviews. Certainly, companies providing these feedback facilities would be foolish not to promote their knowledge by favoring cool hunters and mavens in some way, possibly by discounts on products they agree to review or by giving them the item free of charge. On my own website, NewConsumer.co.uk, I have a cool hunter and maven page, on which information is collected and collated as part of my continuing consumer research.

By identifying and cultivating cool hunters and neighborhood mavens, companies should be able to start a cost-effective buzz going about selected products or services that will enhance sales among New Consumers far more effectively than expensively orchestrated advertising hype. If you can convince a cool hunter or maven about your service or product, you will automatically be selling it not only to New Consumers who trust their judgment, but to all those who pick up a buzz that something new and exciting has hit the streets and rush to catch some of that excitement and action for themselves.

Summary

◆ In an increasingly competitive marketplace offering an ever-expanding abundance of choice, both consumers and producers need the services of cool hunters and mavens.

◆ Cool hunters are alpha consumers, innovators who track down the latest trends and fashions at street level.

◆ Mavens are early adopters who pick up and run with the innovations identified by cool hunters.

◆ There are various types of maven, of whom the least recognized and regarded by manufacturers and marketers are those unpaid, but highly influential, shoppers operating at neighborhood level. Although they may only communicate their views to a few people, their power to make or break new products is considerable.

◆ The manner in which new products and services spread through consumer society is known as diffusion. It starts when cool hunter innovators detect a trend, which is then taken up by mavens (early adopters) who persuade New Consumers (early majority) to follow their example. Following in the rear are the late majority and laggards. By the time these pick up on a trend it is nearing the end of its run.

◆ Cynical New Consumers who pay little attention to expensively created hype are strongly influenced by street-level gossip or buzz. Once persuaded by buzz, however, New Consumers are far more receptive to and willing to be persuaded by hype.

◆ The cycle of innovation is now turning so rapidly that high-cost status symbols can be transformed in just a few months into so-what commodities that are either sold off cheap or even given away.

◆ Manufacturers and service providers need to be continually feeding fresh products into the cycle, so that by the time a trend is passing mavens have something new to spread their buzz about.

6

Involving the New Consumer

Many of the activities that people used to entrust to others they are now doing themselves – transporting provisions in their own trucks, rebuilding their houses ... and managing their own finances. There's something big going on here, this move towards self-reliance, something big and undocumented.

Fortune

Every purchase, whether it involves company-to-company expenditure on raw materials or personal spending on goods and services, consists of three stages: investigation, acquisition and consumption:

◆ *Investigation* involves finding and assessing whatever you want to purchase, anything from browsing the shelves of retail stores to leafing through a catalog, tuning into a TV shopping channel, browsing the internet or making inquiries of potential suppliers.
◆ *Acquisition* is the stage at which you gain ownership of the product or service. It may involve comparing items on the basis of quality and value for money, discussing your needs with sales staff, or even having a free trial to decide whether it meets your purpose.
◆ *Consumption* is the act of using your newly acquired product or service.

Within these three stages there are two key elements – a process dimension (investigation and acquisition) and an outcome dimension (consumption). Despite their scarcities of time and attention, New Consumers are now increasingly introducing a further stage into the process dimension by becoming more personally *involved* in the creation of the product or service they want to purchase:

Investigation   Involvement   Acquisition   Consumption
PROCESS DIMENSION   **OUTCOME DIMENSION**

While it could be argued that every purchase involves at least a small measure of involvement, what I am talking about here often demands far more time and attention than selecting an item off the shelf and paying for it. At first sight it may seem strange, given the scarcity of these resources, that New Consumers are prepared to invest them in this way. But, as I explain in a moment, there are a number of situations in which they are not only willing but also eager to do so.

There is, of course, nothing particularly new about consumers being involved in creating the products they consume. Less than 200 years ago, in the largely agricultural economies and predominantly rural populations on both sides of the Atlantic, self-sufficiency was essential to survival. Most food was home grown, clothes and many other household items were produced entirely or in large part by those who wore and used them, while other goods would be bought from suppliers, such as blacksmiths and cabinetmakers, who were also manufacturers. Larry O'Brien and Frank Harris explain:

> *The system, however Spartan compared with today's retailing system, was already a development on practices common before 1800 which emphasized self-sufficiency and the use of fairs and periodic markets.*[1]

All this changed following the Industrial Revolution as a massive migration of populations from the countryside to towns and cities led to an inevitable decline in self-sufficiency. A rising urban population, buoyant economy and low unemployment created vast demand for new goods and services. These increased the rate of industrialization, encouraging the development of mass production and mass marketing. For a majority of the population, this led to an almost total dependence on the skills and labor of others. In less than a century individuals had changed from active participants in the production of items for their own use to passive purchasers of virtually everything.

Since the early 1980s, the pendulum has been swinging back again as computer technology and the changing desires of New Consumers are combining to produce more active involvement in the production and sale of goods ranging from cars and computers to fashions and radio phone-in programs to the internet.

Why New Consumers Get Involved

Apart from those occasions when, perhaps for financial reasons, there is no choice but to become involved, there are three circumstances in which New Consumers are willing to invest time and attention in making a purchase:

◆ to save time
◆ to gain personal advantage
◆ to increase their enjoyment

Getting involved to save time

Becoming involved at some stage in the sale or production process has the potential to save time in one of two ways. In the short term, it reduces delays in finding and purchasing products to a minimum; and in the long term it ensures that what is bought exactly meets your needs. At its most basic level, involvement means nothing more than taking over tasks once performed by company employees: using ATMs rather than queuing to see a cashier or filling the car with gas yourself instead of waiting for an attendant – on those rare forecourts that still provide such help.

Many New Consumers use self-service stores either when they have no choice, for example when other shops are closed, or when the overall saving of time is still significant. However, many find this so stressful and unpleasant that they race to get the whole experience over and done with as rapidly as possible. Not only does this reduce potential sales considerably, it also means that some retailers may find themselves sidelined by web stores offering speed and convenience with a home delivery service from the comfort of your armchair.

Getting involved for personal gain

With time and attention in such short supply, advertisers and marketers are going to increasingly desperate lengths to persuade New Consumers to become involved with their commercial messages. One way of achieving such involvement, as I explained in the previous chapter, is to offer a reward of some kind, either by making a valuable service available free of charge or paying people to get involved.

Advertisers have often claimed that the most powerful word in any language is 'free'. If you doubt this, consider the success of Dixon's Freeserve, the UK internet service which, within just a few months of being launched, gained a million subscribers and added an estimated £2 billion to the company's market capitalization.

'Free is becoming synonymous with Internet,' comments journalist Peter Martin. 'The combination is synonymous with "hot stock".'

Using a free computer and a free modem, you can now become involved with the internet at no cost, obtaining free software, free news, free e-mail services, free electronic magazines and a free mailbox. You can auction goods for free, read book reviews for free, play free online games and set up a free calendar.

This boom in free services and products, Peter Martin believes, results from the convergence of two business trends. The first is the increasing acceptance by the general public of advertising messages even in areas previously considered private, such as computer screens, rented or purchased videos and even personal telephone conversations. Pioneered by Swedish company GratisTel, the latter service offers free telephone calls to users who are prepared to allow their conversations to be interrupted every two or three minutes by brief commercials, announcing a special discount at the supermarket, a new film, a magazine subscription or some similar product. After ten seconds of hard sell by a young sounding female voice, callers are reconnected. This strategy for involving New Consumers in a wide range of products is expected to reach some ten million subscribers by 2002.

Paying to ensure New Consumer involvement is another strategy being tested by a number of internet companies. CyberGold and MyPoints, for example, pay per response, the former when you visit an advertiser's website and the latter when you click on an advertisement. The San Francisco-based AllAdvantage.com goes even further, seeking to involve consumers by paying 50 cents for every hour they keep an advertising window open on their PC screen, irrespective of whether or not they further involve themselves by visiting the site. The window, known as a viewbar, lets the advertiser know whether or not the consumer is still connected to the internet and changes the advertisements from time to time. The only information that consumers prepared to involve themselves in this way need give the company is their name and the address to which they want their monthly check, capped at 40 hours or $20 per month, to be sent.

Jim Jorgensen, one of the four founders of AllAdvantage.com, says that membership now stands at 1.2 million worldwide, with a further 100,000 joining each week. Not only will the company attract revenue through advertising, it will also be able to market its extensive zip code database, provided by users when they sign up, to other marketing companies. In the future they also plan to pay subscribers who provide additional information about themselves, such as age, income, hobbies and so on.

This will enable the company, and those to whom they sell the information, to create an accurate tastespace for each consumer who becomes involved with the project, so making it easier to target them with advertising information of the greatest relevance.

While giving things away for nothing and paying for involvement are clearly powerful ways of involving consumers, the idea of simply asking them to become involved, without any reward or incentive, might appear a far less viable proposition. Nevertheless, some marketing specialists believe that it could become the most effective form of involvement of them all. Seth Godin, currently vice president for direct marketing at Yahoo!, observes:

> *Traditional advertising and ad banners are based on Interruption Marketing, because they interrupt a television show or a visit to a web site. We've created a paradigm where consumers eagerly give you permission to market to them – and they choose to pay attention.*

Yoyodyne Entertainments, a company he founded, plans and executes marketing campaigns for customers including GeoCities, Bausch & Lomb and Happy Puppy, using e-mails and web promotions based around contests and games. How this works is best explained by describing a promotion that Yoyodyne devised for US tax consultants H&R Block, entitled 'We'll Pay Your Taxes', which generated 46,000 players and 1.5 million hits during its ten-week run. Banners, distributed at popular points on the web, invited people to: 'Click here if you want H&R Block to pay your taxes.' On doing so, interested individuals were taken to H&R Block's site, where they were asked to provide their e-mail address, a request with which 85 percent of callers complied.

From that point on, Yoyodyne used the address to contact subscribers directly, asking trivia questions about H&R Block Premium Tax Service that required the subscriber to examine the company's website in order to find the answers. The dialogue enabled the company to educate interested parties about the services they offered, in return for the chance of winning an attractive prize. The total cost of the campaign, around $60,000, was less than a couple of advertisements in *Time*.

The Firefly Network provides another approach to involving consumers via permission marketing that has the additional advantage of building tastespace maps of participants. Visitors to this website give themselves aliases and supply information about their likes and dislikes.

From these responses an 'intelligent agent', developed at MIT's Media Lab, creates a tastespace that it then matches to the individual's closest tastespace neighbor. Firefly then provides the user with a passport that is used by such business partners as Yahoo! and Barnes & Noble to identify product or service preferences, so providing these companies with information that is both highly relevant and personally involving.

Getting involved to have more fun

While both types of involvement described above may provide a measure of entertainment, any pleasure derived is secondary to the main benefits of saving time or being rewarded. If, in addition to these elements, manufacturers and suppliers can introduce a genuine measure of fun, the involvement of New Consumers and the success of their product or service are virtually certain.

E-Trading, for example, has transformed banking and financial services as more and more private individuals play the stock market from their front rooms. Far more than any profits they make – and losses tend to be a more likely outcome – the lure of becoming involved in cybertrading is the entertainment value of taking part. As Michael Wolf says:

> *They discover that it is fun. Certainly more fun than calling their broker and getting a recording. It has the action of gambling, the thrill of making decisions based on late-breaking news, and the joy of the power to actually do something all by yourself that can affect your financial future.*[2]

There are more and more instances in which involvement not only saves time but also increases the fun of finding and choosing purchases. Take, for instance, putting together an entirely new outfit on the internet, so saving yourself the time and trouble of going around clothing stores. Instead of selecting the goods from catalog pages, shoppers can now test a vast range of clothes and accessories using a virtual reality model of their own body. Systems already in use by companies such as Lands'

End and J.C. Penney offer three-dimensional models to which customers can apply their own measurements before 'trying on' any clothes they are considering buying. These cyber mannequins can be made to match not only each customer's physical dimensions but also their facial features, skintone and hair color. Louise Guay, founder and CEO of Public Technologies Multimedia, the Montreal-based company that developed My Virtual Model, explains the concept:

> *This technology provides the shopper with an electronic mirror. It gives the user the freedom to explore new possibilities in fashion and style.*

An even more personal approach to finding your ideal outfit, developed by Israeli software house Hi-Pic, involves e-mailing or posting a color photograph of yourself wearing only your underwear, or tight-fitting clothing, to any web fashion vendor who uses the system. The picture appears in a virtual dressing room and you can try on clothing by simply clicking through the catalog. It is also possible to involve family and friends in selecting your wardrobe by e-mailing them pictures of yourself in the different styles and asking for an opinion.

Would you enjoy helping to edit the latest book by your favorite author? This has already been tried – to a limited extent – by bestselling American mystery writer Lisa Scottoline. Months prior to the publication of her latest thriller, *Mistaken Identity*, she posted the first chapter on the net and invited the world to have a go at editing the text. Not only did this result in feedback from hundreds of readers, it also provided her with valuable publicity after the press got wind of this unusual invitation.[3]

The same level of involvement will soon extend to editing your own newspapers and magazines. Intelligent agents, primed with your reading tastespace, will scour the net to discover articles, features, news stories and information of greatest appeal to you personally, whether in the fields of general news, sports or celebrity gossip. All this information, complete with illustrations, will be downloaded automatically from the internet each morning on to 'electronic paper'.

Developed by Nick Sheridon at Xerox's Palo Alto Research Center, this 'e-paper' is actually a plastic film containing millions of 'gyricons', tiny spheres that are half black and half white, which reconfigure themselves according to an electric charge to lie either white or black side up. Such 'paper' will provide not only newspapers but whole books just one sheet thick, stock-market quotes that update themselves as you read and magazines with moving pictures.

Music lovers are already involved in producing their own perfect music albums that include only the tracks and artists they most want to hear. Digital audio devices can be connected to the computer and will download an hour's worth of music in around six minutes. At present this often constitutes piracy, which is currently costing the industry some $5 billion a year. Even after newly introduced encryption techniques, designed to prevent illegal copying, have made this all but impossible, the industry will have established websites from which, for a fee, music lovers can legally download their own favorite artists, composers and tracks.

Increasingly, music will not only be bought on the net, but also created there to a consumer's specific requirements. The global music market is predicted to rise sharply over the next few years, with current cassette and CD sales of $346 million rising to $47.5 billion by 2004. This dramatic increase will be largely due to greater involvement by consumers in producing music tailored to suit their tastes and match their moods. Comments *Wired* correspondent Richard Dean:

> *It's ... the first step toward separating music content from the delivery medium. In a world of unlimited bandwidth, music labels have less to offer. It's this shift the recording industry fears.*[4]

Similar innovations will transform the creation of works of art and video productions, enabling consumers to involve themselves in a wide range of creative activities, such as designing posters or pictures on their PCs that they can then display on wafer-thin wall screens. Movie fans will be able to produce compilations of their favorite scenes or performances from vast libraries of digitized films.

A non-internet company that has enjoyed rapid expansion by involving consumers in an enjoyable way is Brush and Bisque-it, which offers a wide range of undecorated cups, mugs, plates and bowls on which purchasers can design and paint their own illustrations before returning them to the company to be fired in its kilns. The result is highly personal but professionally finished chinaware that saves the time it would take to track down exactly the right combination of color and design, while offering an enjoyable leisure activity.

The rise of third places

One of the most basic ways of making consumption more enjoyable is to create spaces where the fun element turns into relaxed, social, encounters, either with friends or among friendly strangers, transforming what may otherwise be an isolating shopping experience into a social occasion.

Booksellers Barnes & Noble and Borders did just that when they created surroundings that were more like a book lover's private club than a supermarket for books. In the center of their stores they established an oasis of comfort and relaxation, with easy chairs and couches, tables and coffee on tap. They also organized lectures, writing seminars and discussion groups, so transforming the process of book buying into the pleasurable experience of buying books. As a result, not only did their sales of new books soar – Barnes & Noble saw an increase of around 18 percent and Borders some 14 percent, against an overall US increase of only 4 percent – but so too did sales of the classics and more obscure titles. New Consumers flocked to these superstores not only in search of something to read but also to relax and enjoy themselves in peaceful surroundings.

The desire by New Consumers to combine consumption with socializing is, in large part, a reflection of our loss of public spaces in towns and cities. Not long ago there were numerous places, including the main street, union halls, market squares, general stores and libraries, where people could meet friends, share the latest news and exchange gossip. Today many have been privatized and so removed from the public domain.

Market squares are increasingly being replaced by shopping malls, where the demands of security require all public areas to be kept under surveillance by closed-circuit television cameras and patroled by uniformed staff. While standing or sitting and chatting is not exactly frowned on, it is hardly encouraged either. Places to sit or congregate are often limited, while piped muzak makes casual conversation difficult.

As a result of these gradual but accelerating changes, a majority of urban young now have only the haziest concept of the public 'sphere'. The idea of being able to inhabit a 'third place', which is neither home nor work, neither completely private nor entirely public, is one that holds great appeal for many New Consumers, providing that they can be provided with an authentic reason for being there.

An exclusive health club offers an example of a third place. This provides an opportunity not only to self-actualize, by improving self-image and self-esteem through physical activity, but to mix with like-minded individuals in attractive and congenial surroundings. Our research suggests that for many health club members it is the unique social atmosphere created by a feeling of being united with others in the authentic pursuit of fitness and health that holds as much appeal for New Consumers as the weight rooms and saunas.

American historian Francis Fukuyama comments:

> *Contemporary Americans, and contemporary Europeans ... are increasingly distrustful of any authority, political or moral, that would constrain their freedom of choice, but they also want a sense of community and the good things that flow from community, like mutual recognition, participation, belonging, and identity. Community has to be found elsewhere, in smaller and more flexible groups and organizations where loyalties and memberships can be overlapping, and where entry and exit entail relatively low costs.*

By involving themselves with companies that encourage enjoyable socializing in their public spaces, solitary New Consumers are able to enjoy being on their own yet in the company of similar friendly people in agreeable surroundings. Much of the success of Starbucks coffeehouses can be attributed to their skill in creating just such private/public environments.

Virtual communities

While the number of companies that can benefit by providing a physical third place is clearly limited, what cannot be done with bricks can often be achieved via clicks – by creating around your organization an internet community of consumers in which many individuals pool their knowledge and experiences.

Behind all the technical hoopla, the internet is essentially nothing more than a way of bringing people together. The first communities were the military and scientific establishments. Today communities can include just about anyone who wants to meet up with other individuals who share a common interest, ideal or activity. Because we always feel more at ease among like-minded people, such communities rapidly build trust, not only among online members but also towards the company responsible for making this safe cyberspace available.

Since the early 1970s, creating relationship communities has proved central to the internet revolution. Chuck Martin stresses their importance to its continued development:

> It is far more important to realize that for all its techno-wizardry the Internet is about people, not components. Where there are people there is always the need for community … it is a system whose sole function is to connect people. It is important to recognize that the Internet doesn't do anything more than that … Whatever the product or service [being sold], it is important to keep in mind that in this environment community rules.[5]

Companies able to create strong and vibrant cyberspace communities will rapidly come to dominate internet business. The secret of developing such a powerful presence has far less to do with building interactive websites than with establishing online communities around online brands.

Joseph Cothrel, research director of Arthur Andersen's Next Generation Research Group, believes that in order to achieve this goal companies will have to 'focus relentlessly on the needs of members' by discovering ways in which they can facilitate and contribute to their needs and interests.

John Hagel and Arthur Armstrong describe four types of virtual communities, each meeting a very different human need:

◆ Communities of transaction, whose purpose is either buying and selling of products and services or exchanging information about commercial activities.
◆ Communities of interest, bringing together people with similar pre-occupations or concerns.
◆ Communities of relationship, providing mutual support and a chance to exchange information for people with a similar disability or health problem, such as ME or cancer.
◆ Communities of fantasy, allowing interpersonal exploration and experimentation.

The extent to which companies are able to meet any of these criteria will, of course, vary enormously. Financial service companies, for example, would probably find satisfying even one of them extremely difficult if not impossible. This does not mean, however, that building an internet community is beyond them, only that a more innovative approach is needed.

They might, for instance, follow the policy long adopted by America Online (www.aol.com), whose 'People Connection' service enables individuals to create their own 'rooms' in which to meet other members of the community worldwide, exchange views, share experiences and discuss topics of mutual interest. These cyberspace rooms can also be used as private meeting places in which to join up with family and friends.

Among the internet's most popular online communities are Geocities (http://geocities.yahoo.com), AngelFire (http://angelfire.lycos.com), TalkCity (www.talkcity.com) and Tripod (www.tripod.lycos.com). The

GeoCities site allows users to develop their own neighborhoods based around shops, chat rooms and space on which community members are able to construct their own web pages.

Another option available to companies unable to develop their own communities is to join forces with other online providers to provide members with access to as wide a range of provision as possible. This 'shared industry interface' approach has the additional benefits of reduced overheads and greater flexibility when adding services. Given the rapidly developing and ever-changing nature of the web, such flexibility can provide a significant commercial advantage.

The UK-based Interactive Investor (www.iii.co.uk) allows investors to exchange views with like-minded investors and also, through their discussions, to exert influence over decisions by fund managers.

The third option is for the company to align itself with an already established virtual community. Sometimes termed inhabitation, this is the approach adopted by Citibank (www.citibank.com), which has branded the 450 well-established special-interest sites set up by the Mining Company (www.miningco.com).

Information Encourages Involvement

There was a time when all consumers knew about products or services was what manufacturers and advertisers chose to tell them. The rapid adoption by New Consumers of information technology has made information more widely available and easily accessible than at any time in history. The availability of information has soared, not only via the net but also through books, magazines, cable TV and videos, which means consumers are almost compelled to become more involved in what they purchase.

If information about the prices and features of a new product is easily available, it makes sense to seek this out before parting with any money. Potential purchasers can now print out a dozen independent reviews of any product or service in moments. But, at the same time, it has also become possible for marketers to learn a very great deal more and more about consumers, to plot their tastespace and then use this knowledge to create new products and services with unique and specific appeal.

In the information era, fewer and fewer goods or services are being created exclusively by either consumers or producers alone, but rather through an intelligent partnership of both. The greater the collaboration between producer and purchaser, the more distinctions between them start to disappear and an entirely new type of relationship, based on co-dependency, begins to emerge.

For manufacturers and suppliers, involving New Consumers provides an opportunity for learning a great deal about their tastespace and so come up with compelling new value propositions tailored and marketed to groups as small as one.

For New Consumers, becoming involved not only leads to greater enjoyment and satisfaction, it results in a feeling that the products or services in whose creation they played some role are more authentic and therefore desirable than off-the-shelf products.

But perhaps the greatest benefit of all is that involved New Consumers are far more likely to invest more of their scarce resources of trust in companies they perceive as being collaborators rather than merely suppliers of products or services.

Why Employees Must Be as Involved as New Consumers

Involvement is a two-way street. In order to have fun when making purchases, consumers must be served by employees who genuinely enjoy and are involved with their work. Research across more than 50 European companies has shown that the most decisive factor in building long-term relationships with New Consumers is for employees to feel a passionate and personal involvement in achieving corporate objectives. As Ken Irons cautions, businesses can only achieve what their workforce wants to achieve:

> *The people who actually provide the relationship have to believe in it before they can deliver it. They have to have the confidence and con-*

viction to carry out their role. They have to believe in what they are doing, not in some abstract way but as a living, real part of their lives.[6]

Summary

◆ Although it may seem paradoxical, given their scarcities of time and attention, New Consumers are often eager to become involved at some stage of production or sales.

◆ Selling involves a process and an outcome dimension. In the past manufacturers often assumed that if the end product (outcome dimension) proved sufficiently pleasing, the manner in which it was sold (process dimension) was much less important.

◆ Apart from occasions when they have no other option, New Consumers will become involved under three conditions: to save time, because they are rewarded for doing so, and because involvement increases their enjoyment of the purchase.

◆ The more enjoyable a transaction can be made, the greater the satisfaction and subsequent trust of New Consumers is likely to be.

◆ Creating a third place where they can relax and socialize can significantly increase both the pleasure New Consumers derive from the process of making purchases and the number of sales made.

◆ New Consumers have greater opportunities to inform themselves about products or companies than ever before. But this is a two-way street, with more information about consumers being available to manufacturers. As a result, many goods and services are now being produced as a collaboration between the two.

◆ To involve New Consumers, employees must also feel actively involved in the production and sales process.

7

Retail Heaven – Retail Hell: Why
New Consumers Loathe 'Doing
the Shopping'

We propose stress could be an important consideration in store switching decisions, and we assume individuals will tend to shop in the most satisfactory and least stressful conditions.
Russell Aylott & Vincent-Wayne Mitchell

Once upon a time, choice was a novelty and going shopping an enjoyable way of exercising that choice in surroundings of luxury and ease. In 1807, the poet and essayist Robert Southey noted:

Shops are become exhibitions of fashion ... When persons of distinction are in town, the usual employment of the ladies is to go a shopping. This they do without actually wanting to purchase anything.

As the century progressed, new developments not only added to the excitement and opulence of retail premises, but made them widely available to people from all walks of life, helping, in the words of Emile

Zola, to 'democratize luxury'. In his novel *The Ladies' Paradise*, set in nineteenth-century Paris, he depicts the department store as symbolizing the 'forward momentum of the Age: the bold new forms of capitalism'.

Mica Nava, a leading academic authority on cultural changes, comments:

> *Department stores were more than just places where merchandise was bought and sold. They formed part of the huge expansion of public space and spectacle which included the great international exhibitions, museums, galleries, leisure gardens and, a little later, the cinema.*[1]

Always at the forefront of innovation, department stores were among the earliest public spaces lit by electricity. This was not only for the convenience this provided to shoppers, but also to enable the creation of dazzling window and in-store displays.

In designing these vivid spectacles, managers sought inspiration from the theater and exhibitions. They regularly staged fashion shows and spectacular oriental pageants featuring scenes from Turkish harems, Hindu temples and Cairo markets.

Photography, one of the technological wonders of the nineteenth century, was used to provide shoppers with the illusion of traveling to distant lands, flying in hot air balloons and even landing on the surface of the moon. In addition to breath-taking displays of produce, stores strove to make the whole shopping experience as pleasurable and as relaxing as possible.

Uniformed doormen welcomed customers and carefully trained and deferential sales assistants attended to their every whim. Inside the store, shoppers were greeted by magnificent galleries, sweeping staircases, ornate ironwork and huge glass domes. Walls were clad in marble and hung with mirrors, parquet floors were covered by exotic Eastern carpets and furnishings were upholstered in silk and leather.

Among a wide range of facilities provided by major city stores were supervised children's areas, toilets and powder rooms, hairdressing salons, ladies' and gentlemen's clubs, writing rooms, libraries, picture galleries, banks, ticket and travel agencies, restaurants and tearooms with live orchestras, extensive roof gardens, and in a few cases even zoos and ice rinks.

Not surprisingly given the level of enjoyment and entertainment they had to offer, these luxurious fantasy palaces were tourist attractions in their own right. 'Visiting the stores during this period became, then, an excursion, an exciting adventure in the phantasmagoria of the urban landscape,' says Mica Nava.

How times have changed!

Picture the scene: a crowded supermarket just before a holiday weekend. Many of the shoppers have driven through congested streets and had difficulty finding somewhere to park.

They have pushed laden trolleys or carried heavy baskets up and down packed aisles, struggled to track down all the items they need, and are now standing in a long queue at the checkout. Ahead is the prospect of carrying everything out to the car before facing the tedious and frustrating journey home.

For most people, 'going shopping' has turned into 'doing the shopping', a chore that has long ceased to be an enjoyable indulgence and has become instead a stressful inconvenience. Research suggests that stress is especially likely when buying groceries and other household staples, domestic tasks that make up about a third of all shopping expeditions.

As Russell Aylott, from the University of Sunderland Business School, and Vincent-Wayne Mitchell, of the University of Manchester School of Management, put it:

> *Grocery store stressors have hitherto been overlooked, despite the fact that unprompted responses from shoppers indicate that grocery shopping is perceived as the most distressing form of shopping.*

Blood pressure and stress

Blood pressure measurements involve two readings. The first, called systolic pressure, represents the pumping pressure of the heart as the chambers contract to push the blood around the body; the second, diastolic pressure, is the pressure in the cardiovascular system as the heart rests between beats. Both increase as the body comes under stress, part of the well-known 'fight or flight' response, which evolved in order to help us survive physical danger.

Systolic pressure tends to be more susceptible to stress, while diastolic pressure gives a more general indication of an individual's cardiovascular fitness. In a healthy young person, normal blood pressure is set at around 120mm Hg systolic and 80mm Hg diastolic. These figures represent the height of a column of mercury (Hg) in millimeters, in a mercurial manometer, the device used to measure blood pressure.

North American insurance companies use an arbitrary figure of 140mm Hg systolic and 90mm Hg diastolic as the upper ranges of normal readings. The New York Heart Association regards anyone whose BP is consistently above these figures as suffering from hypertension.

How Stressful is Shopping?

I have conducted studies in London and New York using male and female volunteer shoppers whose ages ranged from the early twenties to the mid-seventies. To measure stress, I fitted them with monitors that automatically recorded heart rate and blood pressure, two bodily functions especially sensitive to increased stress. In addition, they were equipped with an ultra-miniature video camera, fitted into a pair of sunglasses, which provided a recording of the entire trip.

The chart overleaf shows the effects on one New Consumer, a male in his late twenties, who went shopping in London's congested Oxford Street accompanied by his wife and their infant in a pushchair.

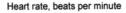

Heart rate, beats per minute

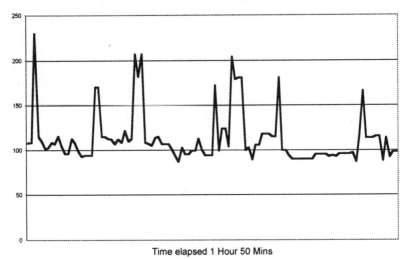

Time elapsed 1 Hour 50 Mins

Figure 2 Stress experienced while shopping

As you can see, both heart rate and blood pressure indicated high levels of physical stress throughout the trip, sometimes to the levels one might expect to find among police officers confronting a rioting mob or combat pilots flying into action. At its best routine shopping tends to create stress; at its worst it can turn your body into a battleground!

With intense price competition leading to wafer-thin margins on many items, it becomes increasingly important to encourage people to browse the aisles in shops and so expose themselves to the temptations of impulse purchases, many of which carry higher profit margins. Stress, however, transforms potential browsers virtually into members of a SWAT team whose sole aim is to dash in, grab what they came for and get out again as fast as possible!

But why should this be so? What is it that so often turns a potentially pleasurable exercise into such a disagreeable experience?

What Makes Shopping so Stressful?

My research suggests that there are four main factors, as well as a number of minor ones, which contribute to shopper stress. These are:

◆ Congestion, in the streets outside the stores and in the aisles.
◆ Delays, caused by looking for somewhere to park, tracking down the items wanted and queuing at checkouts.
◆ Difficulties in locating the items required, often made worse by an absence of assistants or the lack of knowledge of those that are around.
◆ Loud music played to create an 'atmosphere' in some stores.

Additional physical stressors include the premises being too hot or, more rarely, too cold for comfort, or lighting that is so bright it hurts the eyes or so dim it is hard to read product details and labels. Frequent tannoy announcements add to the annoyance for many shoppers, as do confusing store layouts, products moved from familiar locations, inefficient signage and bad product labeling.

The shoppers' state of mind on entering the store also plays an important role in determining how they will react to the above. Difficulties in driving and parking, crowded public transport, bad weather, congested pavements or being distracted or embarrassed by noisy children can generate high levels of stress before any shopping gets started.

It is not just the delays, frustrations or the physically hard work involved in many types of shopping that stresses New Consumers, but in addition the threat to their self-esteem that comes from waiting in queues or being treated with discourtesy. Not that discourtesy always involves the spoken word: a bored or irritated expression, a refusal to make eye contact, or impatient gestures can all convey the impression that consumers are an irritation rather than the store's only source of income. As an example of what I mean, consider the sequence of photographs overleaf, shot using a hidden camera.

◆ Picture one: An elderly shopper, unable to stoop for an item she needs from the bottom shelf of a display, asks one of the staff to help.

◆ Picture two: Without acknowledging her request, giving her a smile or even bothering to make eye contact, the employee strides impatiently towards the shelf, leaving the elderly shopper to follow in his wake.

◆ Picture three: Picking up the item he glances, for the first and last time during that encounter, in her direction, doing so merely to place the product in her hands.

◆ Picture four: Still without uttering a word, he strides back to his task of stacking sandwiches in a display cabinet.

The encounter lasted less than 15 seconds. I have no way of knowing whether or not the woman was upset by such discourtesy. Perhaps she felt affronted and told her friends how rude the staff were in that supermarket. Hopefully she at least took her custom elsewhere. Somehow, though, I doubt it. As she shuffled off down the aisle to complete her shopping, this customer seemed not even to notice the way she had been treated. Probably she was simply accustomed to it. In more than a decade of analysing consumer behavior, I have observed hundreds of examples of discourtesy and even outright rudeness directed against elderly consumers.

Why Old and New Consumers Respond to Different Types of Stress

While both Old and New Consumers become stressed when shopping, exactly what causes that stress tends to differ between them, as the table below reveals.

Old Consumers are most stressed by...	New Consumers are most stressed by...
Their favorite brand being out of stock and having to search for an alternative	Narrow and congested aisles
Product relocation	Checkout queues
Too much choice	Loud music and frequent tannoy announcements
Poor signage	Unhelpful staff
Fear of false arrest	Trolley maneuverability
Information overload	Elderly shoppers or prams blocking their way
Being watched by security cameras	Lack of time
Poor labeling	Insufficient or ignorant staff

From the retailer's point of view, even more important than these different causes of stress are the different ways in which New and Old Consumers react to them.

Because New Consumers are frequently time poor, delays tend to be a greater source of stress to them than for the often less pressured Old Consumer. Faced with lengthy delays at the checkout or problems in locating a particular product, many New Consumers would sooner abandon their purchases and walk out of the store. In a recent survey, seven out of ten of them told me they had done so on at least one occasion, compared with just one in five Old Consumers. Peter Cochrane, head of research at British Telecom, explains:

Often the cost of waiting exceeds the cost of goods, or amounts to a substantial proportion of a total journey's total time.[2]

As a result, despite a price penalty, many New Consumers are switching from supermarkets to smaller convenience stores, where they can develop a closer relationship with employees and often complete the shopping trip far more rapidly.

Old Consumers, even while acknowledging they sometimes find supermarket shopping stressful, are far more reluctant to give up the perceived 'convenience' of supermarket shopping, regarding the stress and fatigue as a price worth paying.

Type A New Consumers

In the early 1970s, two American cardiologists at the Harold Brunn Institute of Mount Zion Hospital in San Francisco, Meyer Friedman and Ray Rosenman, decided the chairs in their waiting room looked worn and needed to be reupholstered. It was a decision that was to have far-reaching consequences for our understanding of role that personality plays in stress and heart disease. Their interest was aroused when the upholsterer pointed out that only the front three inches of their chairs were worn. He asked what it was about their patients that caused them to sit perched on the very edge of their seat.

Intrigued by his inquiry, Friedman and Rosenman searched for some underlying pattern of emotion or behavior that might offer an explanation. In 1974, they published their startling and controversial conclusions. Patients at the greatest risk of heart disease, they claimed, were characterized by:

An action–emotion complex that can be observed in any person who is aggressively involved in a chronic, incessant struggle to achieve more and more in less and less time, and if required to do so, against the opposing efforts of other things or persons.

They described such individuals as possessing a Type A personality, a label chosen, it was suggested, to make it more acceptable to psychiatrists and psychologists, who might otherwise feel hostility towards cardiologists studying a 'psychological' phenomenon. The Type A concept caught the imagination of researchers and produced a host of reports, the majority of which fully supported Friedman and Rosenman's conclusions. In one American study, for instance, 35 out of 50 individuals with coronary heart disease were Type A. Comparable distributions were found in a similar Soviet research project, where 82 percent of heart patients were Type A.

Cardiac specialist Dr Ethel Roskies comments that the debate surrounding the concept of Type A behavior has been 'particularly vitriolic'. This is partly, she suggests, because while most people accept that smoking, lack of exercise and poor diet are bad for our health, almost everything about the Type A person seems praiseworthy to those raised in a striving, competitive western society. Ambition, a need to achieve, a driving desire for success and advancement are, in many ways, rightly valued characteristics. She explains:

Consciously, at least, we know that it is harmful to eat and drink too much, to smoke, to drive instead of walking. But can we really believe it is harmful to be energetic, ambitious, hardworking, and achievement orientated? For many of us, these are virtues learned at our mother's knees!

Three characteristics distinguish Type A individuals:

◆ A strong commitment to work and a great deal of involvement with their job.
◆ A continual awareness of time pressures, always working against the clock to meet urgent deadlines.
◆ A strongly competitive nature.

All these traits could equally well describe a majority of New Consumers. They frequently report having to struggle to retain control over events by being involved and proactive in the marketplace. If that is threatened by circumstances beyond their control, such as unexplained delays, poorly trained staff or insufficient provision of goods, their usual response is to invest further time and effort to 'get things back under control', often resulting in ever rising levels of stress, frustration and anger.

The Type B personality, by contrast, is more laid back, less time pressured, and less concerned to try to exert tight control over events. They are more inclined to 'go with the flow' and are more patient of hold-ups.

Congestion and the Stress of Shopping

Simply being in a large crowd raises one's stress levels above normal. In part, this is because they represent an constant invasion of personal space. This, as is now fairly well known, is an invisible 'bubble' that we each keep around ourselves. The size of this bubble varies according to our nationality, whether we live in the city or countryside and how familiar we are with the other people. Intimate partners are permitted to approach as close as they like, but people we know only slightly or not at all are kept, literally, at arm's length.

When our personal space is invaded by strangers, various body signals are exchanged to make it clear that this is due solely to circumstances, and must not be mistaken for an invitation to intimacy. These non-verbal messages include avoidance of eye contact and maintaining a straight-ahead, 'unfocused' gaze. While useful in some congested situations, for example when traveling on rush-hour public transport, neither is normally appropriate in a crowded store, where one must keep a constant eye on others to avoid collisions.

Congestion is a significant cause of stress for New Consumers, partly because of the extra delays – especially at checkouts – that other people can cause, but also because their strong sense of individuality and independence makes them less happy at being part of a crowd.

What causes shopper congestion?

The most obvious cause of congestion might seem to be that the aisles are too narrow for the number of people using them. In some instances this is the case. Designers of older stores especially either failed to forecast the massive growth in supermarket shopping or were constrained by lack of space in town center locations. Since such premises have long lifecycles, structures tend to be modified and improved rather than rebuilt entirely. Given a fixed amount of space and the obvious commercial pressures to stock as wide a range of products as possible, the scope for widening aisles is clearly limited. In my experience, retailers frequently compound the problem by blocking already narrow aisles with large and often superfluous central displays, which force shoppers into even narrower spaces.

Limitations of space aside, finding the perfect aisle width is far from the straightforward matter it might initially seem. The Plaza on London's Oxford Street, for example, has aisles five meters wide at the entrance, narrowing to four meters, with three meters around the atrium. Given that this mall caters for some 35,000 shoppers a week and stands on a street that sees 37 million visitors a year, peak-time congestion is inevitable.

Modern US malls, by contrast, are built with aisles up to twelve meters wide, designed to create a sense of space and freedom. But the matter of aisle width is not as simple as those examples might make it appear. Not only does congestion in wide aisles appear far worse at peak times, but even when the numbers using them are low, these broad thoroughfares mean that only the retailers down one side can be conveniently viewed and visited. Narrower aisles, even when crowded, enable shoppers to spot items of interest on the other side and cross over to examine them. While there is no easy answer to peak-time store congestion, retailers need to take the problem rather more seriously than many currently seem to be doing.

How shoppers respond to crowds is also influenced by a number of additional factors. As well as narrow and irregular aisles, cluttered shelves and fewer staff create an impression of congestion out of proportion to the number of shoppers actually present. Context is also influential in shaping their response. In a bustling Middle Eastern market, vast throngs merely add to the excitement; the same number of shoppers in a similarly sized supermarket is likely to be perceived by New Consumers, especially, as intolerable congestion.

Why people are shopping also plays an important role in whether or not congestion gives rise to high levels of stress. There are two main types of shopping, task oriented and non-task oriented.

Task-oriented shopping involves shorter, more carefully planned trips. Shoppers usually have a clear idea of what they want to buy and are less likely to make impulse purchases. Under these conditions, crowds tend to be regarded as obstacles to success, especially by time-scarce New Consumers, and therefore as a cause of stress.

Non-task-oriented shopping is recreational, pleasurable and may only involve gathering information without making any actual purchases. In these circumstances, crowds may be looked on more favorably, and may even be seen as adding to the excitement and enjoyment of the trip.

Congestion and the butt brush factor

American retail anthropologist Paco Underhill has identified a special aspect of congestion affecting female shoppers that he terms the 'butt brush factor'. His studies suggest that whenever a woman is brushed from behind, whether by a fixture, merchandise or another shopper, she will quickly leave the store. This is one reason, he suggests, that products intended for women and needing to be closely examined should never be situated low down in a narrow aisle, or close to obstacles – such as central aisle displays – that are likely to force shoppers into even closer proximity. He explains:

> *You can't crowd a woman and think she's going to linger. Watch shoppers' faces in busy aisles ... once they've been bumped a few times, they begin to look annoyed. And irritated shoppers do not tarry; in fact, they frequently leave before buying what they came for.*

New Consumers and the Stress of Choice

Another source of stress more likely to affect New Consumers than Old lies in the area of choice.

Many environmentalists challenge as misleading supermarket claims to offer the widest possible choice. They point out, for example, that of the 2000 varieties of apples grown commercially or for domestic use in the UK, only nine dominate supermarket shelves. Nevertheless, with in excess of 40,000 items on the shelves, many supermarket shoppers are frequently confronted by the need to make important choices. This is particularly true of New Consumers because of their continual quest for novelty and authenticity. According to research by psychologist Irving Janis, when faced with any type of choice the first decision that must be made is whether there is any need to make a change at all.

Take a trivial example. A shopper wants to buy a dozen bottles of fizzy drink for her son's birthday party. Next to the brand he always enjoys she notices a new product that claims to have a fresher taste. Should she buy this instead of her son's favorite?

Old Consumers – more brand loyal and less attracted by novelty – are more likely to reach, almost out of habit, for the familiar drink. The result is a low-stress choice known as unconflicted adherence. New Consumers are not only far more attracted by anything novel but less likely to feel bound by brand loyalty. Rather than choosing the familiar bottle, they will be equally willing to give the new cola a try. Here again we have a low-stress choice, termed unconflicted change.

Now consider a third possibility. Being a New Consumer, this shopper is health conscious and reads labels. While reaching for the favorite brand, she remembers a newspaper report warning that the sweetener in it might pose a health risk. She cannot, however, remember all the details of the article and is not sure if the new drink contains the same sweetener and, if so, in a greater or lesser amount. This thought creates a 'double-bind' dilemma, in which either choice may put her child at risk. Her best answer would be to take the time to reread the article and carefully check the contents labels on both bottles. If neither seems as healthy as she would wish, she can look for a better alternative.

This presupposes that she has sufficient time to make such an informed decision. Given the pressures involved in most task-oriented shopping, this is rarely the case. Under some circumstances, the stress that results can be sufficient to compromise her ability to think clearly. As Irving Janis explains:

> *Warnings that arouse intense emotional reactions can lead to resistance to change, misattributions, erroneous judgments, and defective decisions.*[3]

The stress can, under some circumstances, even lead to a panic-like state called hypervigilance. Here the shopper searches frantically for a way out of the dilemma, rapidly shifting back and forth between alternatives, and impulsively seizing any option that seems to offer a solution.

Beating the Retailing Stress Barrier

Congestion at peak times is often unavoidable, although better store layout and the removal of mid-aisle displays might ease the situation. So too would the presence of what Paco Underhill calls a 'decompression zone' at the entrance to the store. He has found that consumers form an impression of the premises within ten to twenty paces of entering, and that this impression strongly influences their willingness to buy.

A decompression zone, which should extend some five meters into the premises, allows shoppers to slow their pace from a fast street walk to a more leisurely browsing speed. It also makes a crowded shop look roomier and less stressful, while enabling shoppers' eyes to become accustomed to lower illumination levels as their body adjusts to changes in temperature and humidity.

While this zone is sometimes used to display posters and notices by local charities or community groups, there is little point in putting anything of commercial value there since a majority of shoppers will fail to notice it. Studies have shown that when merchandise is moved from front or center to the far end, sales can increase by as much as 30 percent. Signs directing shoppers or promoting special offers also become far more effective if placed deeper in the store.

Once a store has been built without a decompression zone it is usually impossible, or at least commercially impractical, to introduce one. There are, however, other ways in which retailers might make shopping less stressful if not actually more enjoyable. Says Larry Hochman, Air Miles' director of people and culture:

> *As consumers we want to say what matters about service, not have it prescribed by a business. We want control and we want speed and ease of service. We want to deal with individuals who can answer our questions, and who have the confidence to make their own decisions. We want service at the speed of life.*[4]

His views were confirmed in a major survey of consumer opinions that my consultancy conducted in the UK and US on behalf of ICL. Among the recommendations coming from grassroots level were the following.

Greater use of in-store technology to make shopping speedier

Seven out of ten consumers in both the US (71 percent) and UK (69 percent) believe that technology will make shopping easier, quicker and less stressful. The ways in which such technology might help range from greater use of the internet to an in-store system to direct them to the produce they need, allow them to avoid checkouts by self-scanning of barcodes.

Longer opening hours

With increasingly irregular working hours, consumers like to be able to visit a shop at any time. Approximately three-quarters agreed with the statement: 'I find it useful being able to shop outside normal opening hours' (US 77 percent; UK 73 percent).

New procedures for avoiding queues

Standing in line when grocery shopping was rated the single most unpleasant aspect of the task. About a third of North Americans (31 percent) and four out of ten UK shoppers (42 percent) rated queues as their number one shopping hate, followed a long way behind by crowds (US 7 percent; UK 18 percent).

The suggestions given are particularly significant because the interviewers did not present consumers with a choice of possible responses, but allowed them to provide their own responses. Ways of preventing queues ranged from employing more staff and opening more checkouts to greater use of technology.

Home shopping

Unless steps are taken to reduce stress, high street and out-of-town retailers may find themselves losing more and more business to home or office-based shopping, via the internet or television shopping channels.

More than a third of consumers interviewed in our survey expressed an interest in home shopping or home ordering – picking up their groceries later. Just over four in ten (41 percent) of British consumers and 37 percent of Americans agreed with the statement: 'I would be interested in a weekly food shopping service that delivered to my home or workplace, or prepared it for me to collect.'

More radically, a third of Americans (34 percent) and a quarter of UK shoppers (24 percent) would be willing to give up visiting the shops at all were there a reliable alternative method. These proportions agreed with the statement: 'I have always gone out to shop but I would be quite happy not to if there was a more convenient way of doing it.'

This result is particularly interesting because people are rarely willing to volunteer to change. They usually prefer to sample the alternative first, and be won over if it is shown to be a better alternative. In this case, their opinions of some of those who say they would, effectively, give up shopping may have been swayed by experience of home shopping.

Shopping via the office computer also held appeal for many. At ICL's UK headquarters outside Reading, Berkshire, such a system is already in place. Employees can log on to a local supermarket's website and type in their orders, which are then sorted, packaged and delivered to the company's reception area ready to be collected when the day's work is finished.

Those most willing to change their method of shopping in this way were predominantly New Consumers, who also tended to be from higher income groups, had PCs and used the internet on a regular basis. They are more likely to be men than women, and younger rather than older, with the over 55s being most resistant to such innovations. This could, at least in part, be due to older shoppers enjoying the social aspects of shopping and – as a group – being less comfortable with using the net.

For a majority of shoppers, however, an even more direct way of reducing stress and putting enjoyment back into even routine domestic shopping would be a return to the 'pleasure dome' principle that so delighted and inspired consumers at the end of the nineteenth century. This is a strategy that more and more innovative retailers are starting to follow.

Back to the Future – the New World of Entertainment Retailing

Not so long ago, a Victorian shopper transported in a time machine to almost any supermarket or mall would have thrown up her hands in horror, and wondered why on earth consumers paid good money to suffer so much stress and so little fun.

Many present-day consumers obviously thought the same. The number of weekly trips to US malls fell from 2.6 in 1994 to fewer than 1.7 in 1998. Recognizing the threat, an increasing number of retailers are working to transform the whole shopping experience and reclaim some of the glories enjoyed by shoppers a century ago.

Bluewater in Kent, Europe's largest mall which opened in 1999, offers marble and gilt opulence, with spacious colonnades and a massive glass-domed ceiling, equal to anything the department stores of Edwardian cities were able to provide.

But Bluewater's magnificence almost pales into insignificance when compared with West Edmonton Mall, the biggest in the world, in

Alberta, Canada. Constructed in 1986, this gargantuan mall, with four million square feet of retail space and parking for 20,000 cars, numbers among its attractions a full-scale replica of the *Santa Maria*, Columbus's 80-foot-long flagship, a two-block replica of Bourbon Street, a zoo, a church, an 18-hole miniature golf course, an icerink and a night club that can hold 700 people.

As if all this were not enough, West Edmonton also contains Fantasyland, a five-acre water park complete with its own beach and waves, plus the world's highest rollercoaster whose cars travel at 60 miles an hour.

North America's largest mall, in Bloomington, Minnesota, boasts:

Anyone who thinks that the Mall of America is just a big mall probably also thinks that the Grand Canyon is just a big hole in the ground.

Built in 1992, using twice as much steel as in the Eiffel Tower, it covers more of the earth's surface than Moscow's Red Square and could comfortably hold 20 Saint Peter's Basilicas, seven Yankee Stadiums or the entire gardens of Buckingham Palace. Four hundred shops flank 13 miles of aisles, and the mall also contains a school, boxing rink, archery range and, at 76 acres, America's largest indoor entertainment theme park. Here, in climate-controlled surroundings, you can pan an authentic mining sluice for gold and take any claim home with you.

While these last two malls are exceptionally large, they are by no means unusual in their creators' desire to restore elegance and fun to the shopping experience, to become places where one goes to have a good time in addition to buying things, to luxuriate in surroundings that not only inspire awe and excitement but cater for every desire. It is a concept that many modern retailers seem to have forgotten, but one their Victorian forebears would have both understood and applauded. They knew that where people choose to spend their money is far more strongly influenced by their emotions than any intellectual deliberations.

What was true in the nineteenth century remains as relevant today, when many buying decisions depend to an even greater extent on how we feel about the supplier than what we think about the product.

UK retailer Sainsbury's discovered this fact of business life the hard way, seeing its market share take a dive as once loyal customers were lured away by competitors. 'We established ourselves as clinical, methodical, rigorous, professional and very, very precise,' admits marketing director Kevin McCarten.

But research also showed that the company was perceived as overly authoritarian and out of step with the times. 'The emotional attributes of our brand became increasingly old-fashioned,' agrees McCarten, adding that henceforth Sainsbury's would show it cared as much about people as products.

Summary

◆ Shopping has changed from being leisurely and enjoyable to becoming what is often a stressful and tedious chore.

◆ Stressed shoppers spend as little time as possible on the task, so significantly reducing the time spent browsing and the amount of money spent on each trip.

◆ Key stressors include congestion, delays, queuing, lack of sales assistants and being treated with indifference, or even downright rudeness, by staff.

◆ New Consumers may be more susceptible to shopping stress than are Old Consumers due to personality differences between the two groups.

◆ Ways in which stress might be reduced include greater use of in-store technology to reduce delays, longer opening hours, and even relocating retailing from high street to home via the television or internet.

◆ More and more retailers are fighting back by creating environments that recapture the lost elegance and enjoyment of late nineteenth-century shopping. As New Consumers increasingly dominate the marketplace, such tactics may prove even more necessary to prevent a significant loss of business to home or office shopping.

8

New Consumers – New Commercials: Why Television Adverts Must Change or Perish

Mass advertising has lost its ability to move the masses. Technology has given many people more options than they had in the past and created a consumer democracy.

Sergio Zyman, former marketing director for Coca-Cola

Christopher Columbus would have made a perfect television advertising executive. After all, he set off with no clear idea where he was going, when he arrived he didn't know where he was, and when he returned he didn't know where he'd been – what's more, he did it all on someone else's money!

That, at least, is the accusation that an increasing number of influential critics have been laying at the door of the advertising industry, ever since the growing influence of New Consumers started to turn the traditional idea of mass marketing on its head. Over the last decade a consensus has formed among researchers that the power of many television commercials to affect sales ranges from the insignificant to the non-existent. As journalist Jon Rees comments:

> *Some of the most acclaimed and memorable ads of all times have been pretty awful at doing what they were created for: selling product.*[1]

Coca-Cola appeared to have tapped into the spirit of the age when it featured a throng of ethnically diverse teenagers standing on a hill and telling viewers 'I'd like to teach the world to sing.' These commercials became classics and are still fondly remembered 30 years later – yet throughout the campaign US sales remained flat or declined.

More recently, commercials for Miller Lite, featuring boxer Joe Frazier, with the punch line 'Tastes great, less filling', although admired by company employees, distributors and customers, did nothing to aid sales that slowed throughout the period of the campaign. Richard Pinder, managing director of Ogilvy & Mather, explains:

> *The ads can be full of exciting, memorable images, but then there is nothing in the product that there is a link between the two, let alone any reason to buy it.*[2]

To add to advertisers' woes, viewing figures are falling and audiences fragmenting. The final episode of hit comedy series *M*A*S*H*, in 1983, was watched by 106 million people. Sixteen years later, the final episode of *Seinfeld*, rated by many as the greatest sitcom of all time, was seen by 76.5 million – still undoubtedly a vast audience, but a third lower, despite the show's massive popularity.

Compounding this problem is the fact that more and more programs, especially major sporting events and blockbuster movies, are being sold as pay-per-view through premium channels rather than supported by advertising. One almost inevitable consequence is that the quality of free TV will decline sharply, making even less compelling viewing the 90 percent of programs that people watch only because there is nothing better on.

Nor are these the only challenges facing television commercials as the time-and-attention-poor New Consumer rises in influence. Another potentially even more fatal blow to so-called interruption advertising is an innovative piece of technology, known as a personal video recorder (PVR), that is set to revolutionize viewing habits on both sides of the Atlantic. This low-cost set-top box is capable of storing up to 100 hours of programming, against the 8 to14 hours available on conventional video recorders. Even more crucially, because the incoming signal, from whatever source, is digitized, viewers will be able to exercise total control over what they watch. They could, for example, instruct their PVR to record every episode of *Frasier* and any film featuring their favorite star. Furthermore, editing out commercials will merely require clicking a button to instantly jump 30 seconds forward.

By 2004, according to Forrester Research of Cambridge, Mass., some 13 percent of US homes will have a PVR, an adoption rate faster than that achieved by the now ubiquitous video recorder. Within a decade, predicts Forrester analyst Josh Bernoff, only a minority of viewers will see programs as they are broadcast, with most people making recordings and watching when they wish to do so. This means that unless viewers *want* to watch television commercials, they need never sit through another advertisement again. On current form, it seems unlikely that many New Consumers will wish to do so.

In this chapter, I want to consider what can be done to increase the liking for television commercials as a form of communication, not merely in relation to individual features of certain advertisements – presenters, animations, photography, settings and so on – but to television advertising as a medium of communication. To understand how this might be achieved, it will be helpful to step back some six decades to see how it all began.

The Birth of Television Commercials

On 1 July 1941, the first-ever networked TV commercial was broadcast by NBC in New York. An advertisement for a Bulova clock, it lasted 20 seconds and cost $9 to air. Fourteen years later, at 8.12 pm on 22 September 1955, UK viewers saw their first commercial on the new London-only independent television service, a toothpaste advertisement that had won its place in TV history in a lottery against 23 other contenders. An actress named Meg Smith was seen brushing her teeth in the approved manner, 'up and down and round the gums', while a tube of toothpaste burst out of an ice block and the smooth tones of BBC presenter Alex Macintosh exclaimed: 'It's tingling fresh. It's fresh as ice. It's Gibbs' SR toothpaste.'

From such small beginnings has grown an industry that today spends over $100 billion worldwide and, in the UK alone, produces more than ten television commercials a day, every day of the year.

When Bulova aired its first TV commercial, only around 10,000 Americans owned receivers. Less than 20 years later that number was over fifty million and watching television had replaced listening to the radio as the nation's number one leisure activity. In large part this was due to the development of the American advertising industry.

'We molded the environment to fit our need,' Edwin L. Artzt, former board chair and chief executive officer of Procter & Gamble, told a conference in 1994. 'We created soaps, comedy shows, variety shows, and mysteries.'

During the 1950s TV commercials were essentially 60-second dramas with the product as hero, adverts that BBC television producer Nick Barker has likened to extensions of wartime propaganda:

People expected to be told what to do. It was extraordinarily paternalistic, dominated by all these men in white coats.

Not only did viewers patiently sit through commercial breaks, they took notice of what they saw and went out to buy what advertisers told them to buy.

Edwin Artzt describes these early decades of television commercials as the 'Big Brand Era', a period when:

Advertising could create Tides and Tylenols, Pampers and Pepsis, almost overnight, by harnessing the dynamic power of mass audience reach, the drama of moving pictures, and the repetitive force of immense audience loyalty to programming.

By the 1960s the men in white coats had been replaced by far more charismatic personalities – still largely male – as commercials began copying the presentational style of television programs.

Despite these changes, the industry faced growing charges of banality and criticisms of the lack of creativity in many commercials. The audience's love affair, such as it had been, with television advertising was over and the blues were setting in. In an attempt to recapture the hearts and minds of viewers clients stepped up their investment, producing lavish commercials that were frequently far more creatively exciting, and certainly had higher budgets, than the programs themselves. Hollywood directors, some of whom had started their working life directing television commercials, were hired back at exorbitant fees to introduce more exciting images, startling camera angles, zippier soundtracks and increasingly elaborate special effects.

Advertising agency Bartle Bogle Hegarty spent a six-figure production budget shooting 100,000 ft of film off the Gulf of Mexico for Levi's first commercial. Ridley Scott – who made the box office hits *Alien* and *Blade Runner* – filmed a delivery boy pushing his bike up Gold Hill in Shaftesbury, Dorset, to the accompaniment of Dvorak's *New World* in a Hovis bread commercial. For British Airways, Saatchi & Saatchi pulled off a special effects masterpiece when they used *Star Wars* effects specialists to show Manhattan landing at Heathrow airport!

The era of the million-pound commercial had started, and it brought to the small screen an ability to create atmosphere and tell a story using startling visual imagery. Commercials not only made greater use of pictures instead of words to get their message across, but the speed at which those images were shown became increasingly hectic.

While Old Consumers were often confused by these frenetically changing commercials, younger New Consumers were more likely to regard them as attention grabbing and stimulating. Their greater visual sophistication allows them to make sense of rapidly changing images, even complex ones, more easily and comfortably than any generation before them. They are, to use a term coined by author John Caldwell, true televisuals.

Televisual New Consumers

In his 1964 cult classic *Understanding Media*, Marshall McLuhan argued that technological developments lead to new ideas or tools for thinking that result in a change in consciousness itself. His views are echoed by television lecturer Patricia Holland, who comments:

> *The acceptance of developing screen technologies ... has reorganized our mental experience of space and time, no less than the high speed train and the aeroplane previously transformed our physical experience.*

The ways in which New Consumers, especially those under thirty, have 'reorganized their mental experience of time and space' has allowed them to understand the high-speed, visually complex imagery in pop videos, many commercials, programs such as *ER* and *NYPD Blue*, and especially electronic games. The latter, which now form part of the daily leisure of 85 percent of young American males, have proved especially influential in developing superior visual skills, since to progress from one level to the next players have to follow and respond to complicated, rapidly paced visual information.

The high levels of visual sophistication that result permit television and film directors to incorporate more demanding imagery into their productions. This, in turn, helps create an audience for what film critic Tony Rayns has described as 'hyperkinetic pacing'; that is, cutting between scenes so rapidly that many images remain in view for less than two seconds. This is not so-called subliminal imagery, but images that, although shown only briefly, can clearly be seen and distinguished by audiences.

In order to understand the significance of the finely honed perceptual skills of younger New Consumers, we need to take a few moments to examine the way in which separate images and scenes are joined to create a coherent whole.

The Myth of Subliminal Advertising

The notion that what you cannot actually see can still influence you is one of the most profound myths of advertising, and one first popularized as 'subthreshold effects' by Vance Packard in 1957.

Subliminal advertising was the brainchild of one James Vicary, a New Jersey marketing researcher who claimed in 1958 that by inserting the messages 'drink Coca-Cola' and 'eat popcorn' so briefly into a movie that the audience was unaware of them, sales of both commodities could be increased. Later, when unable to replicate or even produce the results, Vicary confessed to having invented the initial study.

By this time, however, the idea of subliminal messages had become widely known through a book, Subliminal Seduction: Ad Media's Manipulation of a Not-so-Innocent America, by Wilson Bryan Key, which sold over two million copies. Although the theories have since been discredited, concern remains among consumers that advertisers are able to 'trick' them into 'buying products without their knowledge and/or conscious opposition since the advertising was being conducted at the subconscious level.'

Cutting rates and average shot lengths

Although there are several ways of joining shots together, one of the most frequent is a straight cut between one shot and the next, either within a scene or between different scenes. The greater the number of cuts, the faster the pace and the greater the emotional energy generated. Studies have shown that the performances of players in fast-paced films are judged as significantly more powerful than those in films with identical performances and the same dialog, but cut at a slower pace. The length of time a shot remains in view is known as the average shot length (ASL) and it has been declining rapidly in recent years.

For maximum visual effect, a shot should be cut at the peak of what is called its content curve, that moment when viewers have understood all the relevant information and are ready to move to the next shot. If a cut is made after the peak has passed audiences become bored, but when the cut comes before the peak many will end up confused and bewildered. The correct psychological point at which to cut from one shot to the next therefore depends both on the complexity of the images and the visual skills of the audience. The growing sophistication of younger New Consumers can be judged by the significant decrease in ASL over the last 30 years.

In 1978, an average 30-second television commercial contained some eight shots, with an ASL of less than four seconds. Today, double or even treble this number of shots may be fitted into the same time frame, leading to average shot lengths significantly shorter than those of the television programs they accompany.

Average shot length and number of camera shots for 30-second TV commercials

Year	ASL (seconds)	Average no. of shots
1978	3.8	7.9
1980	3.4	8.9
1982	3.9	7.6
1984	3.9	7.7
1986	2.9	10.3
1988	2.6	11.5
1989	2.3	12.9
1991	2.3	13.2

ASLs in commercials have been reduced still further since 1991, with some using shots of two seconds or less. At the same time ASLs for some features and dramas have increased, as indicated in the table overleaf, which compares three top-rated US shows with the commercials accompanying them.

ASLs (in seconds) in 1989 and 1991 TV shows and accompanying commercials

	Shows		Commercials	
	1981	1991	1981	1991
Bill Cosby	4.7	6.0	2.5	2.2
Roseanne	4.8	7.9	2.2	1.9
Who's the Boss?	4.9	6.1	2.4	2.2
A Different World	6.1	7.8	2.2	2.8

The visual sophistication of New Consumers has ensured that rapid cutting rates, complex images and complicated story lines are now part of the movie mainstream. In Oliver Stone's *Nixon* (1995), for example, audiences are obliged to follow a tortuous narrative across several time settings, while in the *Thin Red Line* (1999), Terrence Malick tells a conventional war story in a highly unconventional visual and narrative manner. That both films proved to be both box office and artistic successes demonstrates how powerful the influence of visually literate New Consumers has become.

While digital editing systems, such as AVID and Lightworks, have made visual complexity both creatively and financially easier for filmmakers, the structure of some films, such as *The Rock* (1996), *Con Air* (1997) and *Armageddon* (1998), has become so complicated that several editors have to work on them.

In these and many other modern films and television programs, the purpose of cutting is not just to 'punctuate' the images in order to achieve continuity, but to create a desired atmosphere, a technique known as classical cutting.

Classical cutting

In the early 1920s, Russian filmmaker Lev (Leo) Kuleshov carried out experiments into the effects of montage, using clips taken from old films. He juxtaposed shots of a famous Russian actor, Ivan Mozhukhin, with images including a plate of soup, a prison gate, and a slightly erotic scene.

Despite the fact that the actors' expression was unvarying, audiences interpreted it as suggesting a different meaning with each combination.

Known as the 'Kuleshov effect', this demonstrates the power of editing to alter reality, showing that the significance of a moving image lies less in the shots themselves but in the way that editors choose to manipulate them.

I believe that television commercials insufficiently exploit the Kuleshov effect, which is susceptible to scientific analysis and prediction, not because those who make them lack either the skill or the inclination to do so, but because their hands are increasingly tied by cautious and frequently unimaginative clients.

Putting on the style

As the running time for commercials has fallen from 60 to 30 then 15 seconds, and as the pace of many has become increasingly frenetic, television screens grew increasingly cluttered with advertisements, promotions and programs, jostling for the attention of increasingly jaded viewers. To make themselves noticed in this tumult and to keep viewers' fingers from straying to their channel changers, television commercials and even many programs became ever more stylized. John Thornton Caldwell, of the California State University–Long Beach, observes:

> *Television has come to flaunt and display style. Programs battle for identifiable style-markers and distinct looks in order to gain audience share within the competitive broadcast flow.*[3]

One way of catching the eye of New Consumers is to make commercials seem more authentic by giving them a documentary-like feel. This is often achieved by using techniques pioneered by *cinema vérité* (a form of documentary filmmaking), with handheld cameras and directly recorded sound appearing to document events as they unfold. There has also been a move by a few agencies and directors to use black-and-white rather than color footage in order to create a greater impression of authenticity and actuality.

The focus of some commercials has also shifted to portraying 'real-life' characters in 'real-life' surroundings to permit a greater sense of empathy between viewer and viewed.

While the fact that this creates many striking and memorable images is beyond dispute, for many in the industry there remains a question-mark over whether or not rapidly paced advertisements work. When Mapes and Ross, a North American firm specializing in measuring the effectiveness of television commercials, conducted research into this subject in 1987, they discovered a steady decline in recall and persua-siveness scores as the number of camera shots increased.

Performance measured by the number of camera shots in a 30-second commercial

Number of shots	Index of Persuasion [Average = 100]	Index of recall [Average = 100]
1–5	110	115
6–8	104	102
9–12	110	100
13–19	84	95
20+	81	83

As you can see, once the number of shots rises above 12 within the 30-second commercial, both persuasive power and recall decline. In their influential 1993 report on shot length, James MacLachlan and Michael Logan comment:

> *The data suggest that many advertisers are loading their commer-cials with too many camera shots, and persuasion and recall are suf-fering as a result.*

While this may have been true at the time, my own research suggests that this assumption no longer applies to most younger New Consumers, who not only prefer rapid cutting rates but are far more likely to pay attention and be persuaded by them.

The Genius of TV Commercials

Even those who dislike and always try to avoid television commercials will concede that, no matter how banal their message, many are master-pieces of story telling. In half a minute they may offer viewers heroes and villains, drama, fantasy, humor, excitement, cliffhangers, denouements, conflicts and romances. Given the amount of skill, talent, dedication and even devotion that goes into the creation and production of a television advertisement, what else needs to be done to ensure that visually literate New Consumers will still choose to tune in and pay attention?

This is a question to which my consultancy has been seeking answers for more than a decade, using a technique developed in our laboratory that we term Mind Scan. Starting in the late 1980s with experiments conducted at the University of Sussex, we have been using Mind Scan – a modified form of EEG (electro encephalogram) – to record electri-cal activity in the brains of scores of subjects while they watch a wide variety of television commercials. You will find a full description of this work in the appendix.

My purpose has been to discover whether by studying the brain pat-terns of viewers while they watch commercials in their own homes, it is possible to measure how they respond to the advertisements they see.

The information–image dimension

Television advertisements may be thought of as being located on a con-tinuum, with entirely information-focused commercials at one end and those seeking solely to evoke an emotional response, image-focused commercials, at the other.

Information focused   Image focused

Information-focused commercials are product oriented. They provide facts and figures, demonstrate features and make explicit claims in a rational, logical and factual manner. The message is communicated more by words than by images, with characters and/or a voiceover clearly describing the benefits of the product advertised.

Image-focused commercials seek to produce a visual impact with little, if any, factual information being communicated. The images chosen range from an evocation of 'traditional' values to the highly abstract, even fantastic, while styles are emotive and entertaining.

While some commercials are positioned at one extreme of this information–image continuum, many more combine features from both. As Alan Branthwaite and Alan Swindells, of researchers Millward Brown International Swindells, suggest:

> *These may be the most effective. Communicating something original to naive viewers and constantly reminding consumers of product options, but doing so in a way which is continually interesting and entertaining. By this means they blend the processes involved for the viewer.*

As with rapid cutting rates, my research suggests that while this applies to a majority of Old Consumers, with younger New Consumers such a mixture of information and imagery significantly weakens the commercial's impact. As television producer Nick Barker explains, many viewers:

> *have grown up from being deferential children to becoming highly promiscuous consumers who view the world with great lashings of irony.*

This causes them to distrust advertisements that appear to soft soap them as profoundly as those with a stridently hard sell.

Provided a commercial is entertaining they may be prepared to accept a mixed message, but in most cases the switch from pure images to pure information or vice versa results in a fall in attention combined with distrust and dislike for the commercial and the product or service being advertised.

Creating Commercials that are Likeable and Credible

One of the most successful TV shows of 1998 in the US was a 30-minute program about Sobakaws, Japanese pillows stuffed with buckwheat husks that are claimed to relieve neck pains. Although this seemed little different to any other lifestyle show, the $250,000 program was, in fact, an infomercial – a form of advertising, sponsored by the manufacturer, that blurs almost to invisibility the line between a normal program and a paid-for promotion.

Of all the factors that go into creating an effective infomercial, two of the most crucial are that it should appear both likeable and credible – two of the routes to authenticity. The Sobakaws show, for example, was co-hosted by Jennilee Harrison, star of the popular sitcom *Three's Company*, while to add credibility to the medical claims the co-host was a doctor of oriental medicine.

The importance for television commercials of being liked if they are to persuade successfully was first demonstrated in 1985 by the US-based Ogilvy Center for Research and Development. After examining 73 primetime commercials, spanning a broad range of fast-moving consumer products, they concluded that viewers who liked an advertisement 'a lot' were twice as likely to be persuaded by the message as those who felt emotionally neutral. Mike Bridgwater, former director of research at the Ogilvy Center, comments:

> *Likeable advertising has an impact on persuasion because a likeable commercial affects the emotional component of our attitudes towards the brand.*[4]

Liking for the commercial creates a positive halo around the product, while dislike, even of the most trivial aspect of the message, risks significantly reducing its power to persuade. Some in the advertising industry argue that there is no need for viewers to like an advertisement so long as they recall the brand. Soap commercials, they point out, are widely disliked by most people but still help to sell a great deal of washing powder. While there is some truth in this view, there are two compelling reasons for a likeable advertisement usually proving a surer passport to persuasion – especially among New Consumers: they are also seen as more credible and the product will appear more authentic.

Liking increases credibility

In an early experiment demonstrating the close association between being liked and having your message regarded as credible, an actor was employed to beg for money at New York's Grand Central Station. On different days he appeared dressed smartly, casually or shabbily dressed, but his hard-luck story remained unchanged. He had lost his wallet and needed a few dollars to get home. As the neatly suited business type, with whom hurrying commuters could most easily empathize and therefore find likeable, he collected $513 in a single day. Many well-wishers even insisted that he take twice the money asked for so that he could have a drink and get over his upsetting loss! Wearing smart but casual clothes he managed to raise $150, but when shabbily dressed his takings plummeted to just $10 for a full day's begging – and nobody offered him a drink. Dislike for his appearance led to his tale of woe lacking almost all credibility.

The importance of being credible

Research into the impact of credibility in advertising has shown that as a general rule, the more credible the source, the more likely naturally distrustful New Consumers are to be persuaded by it. For them, a credible third-party endorsement significantly increases authenticity.

It is essential, however, that the spokesperson's appearance in the advertisement does not diminish their credibility. When US TV newscasters Linda Ellerbee and Willard Scott made a commercial for Maxwell House coffee in a set resembling a news show, they were criticized for subverting their own journalistic objectivity. Since their credibility for the brand depended on their authority as objective television reporters, this may well have resulted in their message being judged as less persuasive.

Liking, credibility and paying attention

In Chapter 3, I explained how the amount of attention we are prepared to devote to an advertisement depends on which one of five time shifts we are in when it is presented. Within these varying attention spans, the extent of our liking for and the credibility we afford to television commercials also influences the amount of attention paid.

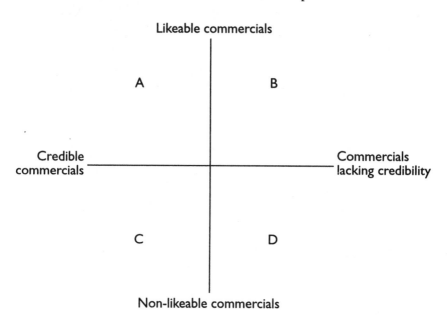

When watching a TV commercial we place it, often without being consciously away of the fact, into one of these four boxes, a judgment that subsequently significantly influences the amount of time and attention invested in it.

◆ Box A (likeable and credible) – the vast majority of advertising, public relations, retail displays and signage seeks to position products or services here. While such messages attract the attention of a broad spectrum of the population, they tend to hold somewhat greater appeal for Old than New Consumers.
◆ Box B (likeable but lacking credibility) – into this box come many

forms of hype, celebrity puffs and press releases. While likeable television commercials are equally likely to catch the eye and hold the
attention of consumers, trusting Old Consumers are more inclined
to be persuaded by them than are sceptical, and often better
informed, New Consumers.

◆ Box C (non-likeable but credible) – while the majority of television
advertisements strive to be as likeable as possible, there are occasions
when advertisers seek to shock viewers by a vivid depiction of cruelty, violence or brutality. Until recently, advertisers tended to avoid
this box, which was more the domain of 'propaganda' messages
intended to outrage people into taking some form of action – those
designed to raise awareness of issues like cruelty to animals or child
abuse, social injustice or the aftermath of natural disasters. Within
the past decade, however, mainstream advertisers have been producing more advertisements whose images and message are uncompro-
mising. While a majority of Old Consumers decry such commercials,
they have an appeal for many younger New Consumers. Although
shock tactics certainly capture the attention of those who might
otherwise avert their gaze from the subject matter in question, the
negative emotions aroused can lead to the message being
misunderstood.

◆ Box D (non-likeable and lacking credibility) – remarkably, since it
appears such infertile ground, a great number of television commercials can still be found in this category, perhaps the most frequent
examples being those for soap powders. While these may help
impress a brand name on Old Consumers, the most likely reaction
from New Consumers is either to change channels or to zap through
the commercial.

New Consumers – New Commercials

Only the most complacent of advertising or television executives would
deny that the TV commercial in its current format is in crisis. Television
audiences are fragmenting into smaller and smaller groups, viewing figures are in decline and advertisers need to discover other, more direct

ways of getting their messages across to New Consumers, using everything from mailings to the internet. At the same time, creativity and innovation in commercials are under pressure from reduced budgets, overly cautious clients and an absence of compelling research methodology.

More than half a century after Bulova splashed out $9 to advertise its clock to a potential audience of 10,000 US viewers, time is running out for traditional television advertising. If commercials are increasingly ignored or wiped unseen from recorded programs while those that are still watched make little or no impact on sales, it cannot be long before companies begin to wonder whether even $9 is too high a price to pay.

Some argue that television commercials have no need to change radically – that it does not even matter whether or not audiences consciously pay attention to them since, by sheer repetition alone, they will still succeed in getting their message across. Andrew Ehrenberg, professor of marketing at London's South Bank University, points out:

Most advertising is not trying to sell. It's just maintaining your position in a competitive market. It's about reminding people and keeping brands salient to people, so that they go on asking for Coke rather than Pepsi, or Bingo rather than Bango.[5]

Martin Sorrell, chief executive of WPP, the world's second largest advertising group, makes an extremely valid point:

Television still remains the preserve of those people who want to reach the largest number of people in the shortest amount of time.[6]

Sceptics will also point out that while virtually every television innovation from the remote control to the VCR has been claimed to sound the death knell of interruption advertising, the growth of commercials continues regardless. Even with a myriad of media competing for their attention, the average viewer continues to spend some three hours each day watching TV.

While this is true, there is certainly no room for complacency. In addition to threats from new technology, there is the steady proliferation of channels, the development of niche markets and the growing number of alternative advertising channels to consider. Given the rapidly increasing influence and financial muscle of New Consumers, it is clear that many aspects of television advertising must change, and change rapidly, if commercials are to be viewed at all, let alone persuade this time-pressed, distrustful, demanding and cynical audience.

On the basis of my own and other studies I offer the following seven suggestions regarding the form these changes might take.

More and more sophisticated research

Many in advertising – especially creatives – will throw up their hands in horror at this suggestion and insist that their industry is already over-burdened by research. While this is certainly true, much of the current, and costly, research methodology is, to echo Macbeth's words, 'full of sound and fury, signifying nothing!'

Methods for testing viewer response, for example, are often both crude and intrusive, with people being shown commercials under conditions significantly different from those of viewers in their own homes. Subjects evaluating commercials may be asked to use a lever to indicate which parts of an image they find the most interesting. This compels them to focus on specific aspects of individual shots rather than viewing the commercial as a whole. Similarly, focus groups and paper-and-pencil-based research only generate a *post hoc* series of responses that may bear little or no resemblance to intellectual and emotional reactions while viewing the advertisement.

To compound the problem, responses to commercials, whether positive or negative, often operate below the level of awareness. While studying brain patterns of women watching an advertisement for the perfume Monsoon, for example, we detected apprehension and anxiety during one particular sequence. This showed a man chasing a woman through a storm-lashed jungle, catching her and swinging her around. The clearly ambiguous nature of these images – an ambiguity enhanced by the choice of camera angle and lighting – resulted in significant unease among younger, female New Consumers. This distress only vanished when it was clear that the woman was in control of the situation and eager for the man's embraces. My researchers and I believe that a resurfacing of such anxiety, which operated below the level of conscious awareness and was not mentioned by any of the women themselves, might have caused them subconsciously to dislike the product and so discourage them from purchasing it.

Research often meets with considerable hostility and resistance from agency 'creatives', who complain that it causes clients to reject truly creative work and fall back instead on the familiar and the mundane. This is a view with which I sympathize, but while intuition and experience will always have a vital role to play when deciding what commercials will work and which are best left on the drawing board, so too should more sophisticated research. Graham Lancaster, chairman of PR firm Biss Lancaster, suggests:

> *The problem perhaps is that there is not enough research or not enough research of the right type. Perhaps the anti-research types feel that marketing and advertising decision making is different. That like Mozart they have divine inspiration and just have to write the notes down. And perhaps they are plug wrong.*[7]

Commercials in unexpected places

Given the scores of choices available for virtually anything we might want to buy and the number of advertisements, around 3000 each day, competing for our limited attention in the New Economy, advertisers must start addressing New Consumers as individuals or in smaller and smaller groups.

Instead of commercial breaks, some advertising and television companies are suggesting that the problem of zapping through commercials could be solved by running them as banners alongside programs or using logos in the corner of the screen. In my view, both methods would be counter-productive because they would alienate New

Consumers. There are many other places where commercials might be displayed in such a way that they would not only be watched but welcomed by consumers.

Towards the end of 1999, for example, UK supermarket chain Sainsbury's launched Europe's first-ever checkout video, using flat screens positioned just above the tills. Different programs, ranging from sport highlights and cartoons to new film releases, were shown at the various checkouts so that customers could choose their favorite. The idea, a spokesman explained, was to keep children quiet while their parents waited in line. But he added: 'We believe technology to improve the shopping experience is one way forward.'

Given the rapidly falling costs of flat-screen technology, we could have loyalty cards fitted with watch-sized TV screens that would guide consumers around stores and flash up news of special offers and promotions. Larger screens could be fitted on to supermarket trolleys, showing consumers where items they require are located and adding commercial messages, perhaps interspersed with cartoons and sports to entertain children while their parents shop.

Although the internet is vastly hyped as the advertising medium of the future, and spending in 1999 was around $3.2 billion, it is far from the pot of gold that some companies seem to believe. Numerous studies have shown that the vast majority of web surfers ignore banner advertisements, clicking on fewer than one in a hundred and being unable to recall the last one they did click.

In an attempt to catch their fleeting attention, some advertisements are becoming flashier, using animations, embedding voice, music or other sounds in banners and even video. V-Banners from InterVU, for example, produces online advertisements with short digitized clips.

An even more radical approach is so called interstitial advertising that interrupts users without warning. One type, known as Superstitials, sneak on to idle computers, store themselves on the hard drive and then commandeer a portion of the screen to display their messages. Although many users complain bitterly about such intrusions, media buyers and marketers claim it is only by becoming this intrusive that internet advertisements are able to get their messages across. In the short term such attention-grabbing tactics appear to pay off, results suggesting that they are better at converting surfers into buyers than traditional forms of web advertising. In the longer term, however, New Consumers' hostility to their time and attention being hijacked in this way is likely to lead to increasing rejection of such messages.

A more fruitful long-term route for both TV and the internet is likely to be paying viewers and computer users to watch commercials, either in cash or by offering some other form of inducement.

Faster, slicker, more visually enjoyable commercials

The writers of *Max Headroom*, a 1980s television series, came up with the idea of blipverts, television commercials compressed into five-second 'blips'. These proved so persuasive that viewers rushed to buy whatever they advertised. Blipverts had one unfortunate side effect, however – they caused viewers' brains to explode!

That difficulty aside, if blipverts ever became a practical reality there would be no shortage of advertisers eager to use them. Not only would they be far cheaper to air at prime time, but time-poor New Consumers are more likely to pay attention for five seconds than for thirty, and are perfectly capable of making sense of what is happening on the screen.

In 1978, a leading advertiser raised the possibility of advertisements lasting just one second. In 1998 his prediction was made good when US company MasterLock screened a number of second-long commercials during the Superbowl – a prime slot with airtime costing up to $1 million. So while blipverts will probably remain in the realm of science fiction, 'flashverts', as one might call them, will probably become increasingly common.

Even faster pacing and greater use of images, rather than words, to communicate ideas and generate emotions will help create sharp, stylish commercials that leave the viewer stimulated and attentive.

Recognize social changes

Western society is ageing and minorities are growing in economic and social importance. Yet advertising in general, and many television commercials in particular, seems to be locked into a social reality that, even two decades ago, was highly debatable. The mainly white, middle-class families, based on heterosexual couples, who still predominate alienate a significant proportion of their audience, who are offended by the subtext of their messages. Minority groups such as single parents, people with disabilities, ethnic minorities, couples in mixed-race relationships and gay men or women often feel that their own values and lifestyles are being dismissed and diminished.

In the US, companies devote less than 2 percent of their total advertising spend to Hispanic and Asian Americans.[8] In 1998, according to the Association of Hispanic Advertising Agencies, spending on Latino advertising was $1.8 billion against a total spend of $186 billion. This is despite the fact that Hispanics account for 7 percent of the country's total consumer spending, at around $458 billion. Although the disposable income of Asian Americans is lower, their median salary – at $46,695 – is higher than any other racial group, including whites.

In the UK, although the over-sixties comprise almost a quarter (21 percent) of the population, they are vastly under-represented both in television commercials and mainstream programming; for example, they comprise only 6 percent of the characters in soap operas, dramas and comedies. As Sally Greengross, director general of Age Concern, comments:

> *Programme makers ignore older people at their peril. By continuing to under-represent older people on television they are also overlooking the power of older people as customers.*[9]

The same can be said of gay men and women, who seldom feature in television advertising and frequently have fun poked at them if they do appear in programs. Such neglect and stereotyping is not only socially divisive but commercially foolish, since it causes companies to ignore a lucrative niche market comprising consumer-conscious males, who seldom have any dependants and whose total annual disposable income is estimated at £10 billion.

The risk of alienating this influential minority group was illustrated when the Bank of Scotland outraged UK gays through an ill-judged venture with the homophobic US evangelist Pat Robertson. After protests led to private accounts being canceled and major institutions threatening to take their business elsewhere, the bank withdrew from the deal, apologized profusely and set about the lengthy process of winning back the lost 'pink pounds'.

Even when they manage to avoid alienating large groups of potential customers, commercials may miss the point by targeting the wrong type of consumers. As an example of lack of relevance, Richard Pinder of Ogilvy & Mather cites small car advertisements:

> *Three quarters of all small cars are bought by the over 55s. But almost all small car advertising is aimed at people in their 20s. Advertising succeeds when it ... talks to the target audience in a way they find relevant.*[10]

Avoid mixing information- and image-focused commercials

As I pointed out earlier, commercials that include both image-focused and information-focused elements are disliked and distrusted by many New Consumers. It would be more effective to provide factual information in an entertaining, stimulating and visually appealing manner. Selling by telling people things they want or need to know is a relatively undeveloped area of advertising, but one which New Consumers, with their strong desire to remain involved and informed, would welcome.

Similarly, purely image-focused commercials, provided that those images are exciting, compelling and original, are likely to command attention.

Mainstream programs with interactive commercial messages

At the moment having a toll-free number to call if you want more information about the product or service being advertised is about as interactive as television advertising becomes. In the very near future, however, television commercials will not only become fully interactive but are likely to be incorporated into mainstream shows.

They might, for example, be presented as a soap or sitcom without any overt selling, but with virtually every product that features being available for purchase. All an interested viewer will have to do is point a device similar to a channel changer at the screen to call up details of the price, product information and availability. A further click and the goods would be ordered and shipped for delivery. Fans of the TV show *Baywatch*, for example, who took a fancy to owning a replica of Pamela Anderson's famous red swimsuit, would only have to point and click for the costume to be ordered and despatched. The same could apply to any number of items in shows, from cars to clothes and furnishings to gadgets.

The shape of things to come can be previewed at AsSeenIn.com, which allows viewers to prowl around the sets of such popular US TV shows as *Any Day Now, Charmed* and *7th Heaven*. The site includes virtual set tours of different locations. Clicking on items of interest takes the viewer directly to an appropriate retailer.

In *7th Heaven*, for example, a click on the Mary and Lucy's Room box takes the viewer directly to a photograph of their bedroom, around which one can roam with a mouse pointer, enlarging any items of possible interest. A reproduction antique oil lamp on the bedside table caught my eye and a click took me directly to the website of the retailer, a Taiwan-based company called Fantasy Lighting.

Limited though it is at the time of writing, the powerful idea behind AsSeenIn.com could, in the near future, have done for traditional television commercials what Henry Ford did to the horse and cart, since association with celebrities always enhances sales.

This even applies when the celebrity is a fictional character, as the enormous success of product placement in the Bond films demonstrates. *GoldenEye*, for example, was used as a launch pad for BMW's Z3 Roadster, which featured in the film before going on sale in the UK. By the time the car became available, order books had to be closed after 6000 customers had queued up to buy it.[11] Sales of the £1000 Omega Seamaster, which replaced 007's Rolex, rose by 40 percent in the UK alone after the film's release. The Italian fashion house Brioni, which supplied handmade suits for both *GoldenEye* and the most recent Bond, the $70 million *The World is Not Enough*, saw US sales skyrocket.

Ironically, movie directors may even use product placement as a way of giving their films an air of authenticity. This was the motivation behind the product placement in Stanley Kubrick's *2001: A Space Odyssey* (1968), in which the director included actual brand names such as PanAm and the BBC to increase the feeling of realism.

More psychologically persuasive commercials

By combining knowledge of individuals' interests, obtained through tastespace analysis, with psychological insights gained through better understanding of brain processes, it will soon be possible to develop far more persuasive commercials than any currently broadcast.

What I am talking about is not any form of subliminal manipulation, but images assembled in such a way as to trigger a desire to buy in the mind of those viewers at whom it is targeted. To some this may seem a chillingly Orwellian prediction – and perhaps it is. But given the commercial pressures on companies and the New Consumers' scarcities of time and attention, there can be no doubt that several major advertising agencies are already researching such possibilities.

A series of commercials for Johnnie Walker whisky, released at the end of 1999, sought to use an emotional approach. What made these advertisements unique was the fact that there is no sign of the product. Instead we see Harvey Keitel, circled by lions, striding purposefully across a Roman coliseum towards a wall in the center of the area while describing his feelings of vulnerability as a young actor. When he pushes the wall it tumbles over and the lions disappear.

'You learn to overcome your fear or spend your life in the wings,' he announces. The screen then fills with Johnnie Walker's Striding Man logo and the message 'Keep Walking'.

Oblique, aspirational advertisements such as these that seek to link a product with personal attainment – another shows French tightrope walker Ramon Kelvink, walking between two New York skyscrapers – are likely to become increasingly popular as global corporations such as Coca-Cola, Nike and Kodak try to build emotional bonds with their brands. Nigel Bogle is chief executive of the UK advertising agency Bartle Bogle Hegarty that created the Johnnie Walker commercials. He says:

> *The desire to make progress is one of mankind's fundamental and instinctive drives. The 'Keep Walking' campaign will not only portray progress but inspire it … it's about achievement, not conspicuous success. It's remarkable how quickly consumers around the world get the idea.*[12]

While this type of approach, with its emphasis on self-actualization, may well hold greater appeal for significant numbers of New Consumers than more direct 'sip and savor' advertising, its effectiveness must still be in doubt. Not so much because the commercial is at fault but because, unless the product – whether a drink, a running shoe or a film – is perceived as having intrinsic authenticity, the effect among New Consumers is likely to be negligible. Furthermore, these cynical and distrustful viewers may well reject any message that appears to turn into a commodity that which they hold most dear, their own achievements.

Summary

◆ Fragmenting markets, niche consumers and the decline in mass enter-tainment are presenting television commercials with one of the greatest challenges they have ever faced.

◆ Younger New Consumers are extremely visually sophisticated and can understand complex images presented extremely rapidly.

◆ These 'televisuals' are also able to follow a complex narrative even when images are rapidly changing. Indeed, they often pay greater attention and show better recall for such visually challenging commercials. While a fast cutting rate reduces persuasiveness and recall among Old Consumers, it generally has the opposite effect on New ones, endowing the com-mercial with energy and impact.

◆ New Consumers are highly sensitive to any subtext in an advertisement and some commercials may lose much of their impact, or even work against the product being marketed, through such unintended messages.

◆ Commercials should, in general, strive to be as likeable as possible, since this will enhance the credibility and authenticity of the message.

◆ While intuition and the skills of creative minds are essential to produc-ing effective television and screen advertisements, more empirical research could help to develop more effective commercials while weed-ing out likely duds at an early stage.

◆ Within the next few years commercials must undergo radical changes in order to survive, not merely changes in terms of how they are shot and edited but also in the places they are shown.

9

Winning their Hearts and Minds: Authentic versus Pseudo Loyalty

Consumers have been transformed from loyal, reliable, and predictable patrons into transients – here today, flitting across the street tomorrow.
Joan Pajunen and Susan O'Dell, The Butterfly Customer

Before the onrush of New Consumers transformed the marketplace forever, major companies might have been compared to majestic ocean liners. Splendid and monolithic in their size and power, they steamed easily and confidently through the fiercest economic storms. Today, many of those same corporations are more appropriately likened to two castaways clinging to either side of a continuously spinning barrel. As one snatches a breath so the other is plunged beneath the waves before the barrel spins him up to the surface again. That is the reality: limited periods of success before hard times come around again, with companies constantly obliged to adjust to new demands as their swiftly rotating barrel briefly raises them above the turbulent commercial ocean.

For manufacturers and suppliers this swirled order represents the downside of the fast-moving, information-based New Economy.

Globalization means that production facilities need not be permanently located in any one country but can be moved to wherever labor is cheapest or government regulations the least restrictive. In a similar fashion, the loyalty of New Consumers flows to whoever has the best ideas and the most rewarding innovations.

The cherished goal of ambitious marketing executives is now to win the lifetime loyalty of those consumers by offering products and services superior to those on offer from their competitors. As one described it to me, to 'sell products that do not come back to customers who do!'

This has resulted in two courses of action. The first, in which many companies – especially the Japanese – have been highly successful, is to continuously improve quality while at the same time reducing prices.

The second has been to become more customer focused in the hope, and expectation, of generating long-term loyalty. This has met with much less success, for two reasons: notions of what it takes to satisfy customers are frequently confused and limited; and a mistaken belief that provided customers are satisfied with the goods and services available, their loyalty can be taken for granted. Unfortunately, satisfaction usually results in only short-term pseudo loyalty rather than long-term authentic loyalty.

A survey among 3000 marketing directors in top UK companies by Smith Bundy and Partners found that while an overwhelming majority regarded customer care as essential, many paid little more than lip-service to the idea. Fewer than a quarter of the companies surveyed made any attempt to measure customer satisfaction. More than half emphasized product quality and competitive pricing as their main strategies for ensuring loyalty, regarding as secondary considerations such aspects of service as the speed with which telephones were answered, goods delivered and complaints dealt with. Relationship marketing, designed to target specific products and services to individual customers, was consistently rated as an 'insignificant' aspect of customer care programs. Yet research shows that neither quality nor pricing is the chief reason for customers taking their business elsewhere. Only one in seven consumers changes suppliers as a result of dissatisfaction with quality and just one in ten is tempted by lower prices. More than two-thirds, however, remove their custom as a result of 'an attitude of indifference' on the part of their suppliers.

Companies have focused their efforts on creating customers who are merely satisfied with the treatment they have received. Although the resulting behavior might suggest that the consumer has become loyal, because their emotions are never engaged they will defect to competitors without a second thought or a backward glance.

Are New Consumers Irredeemably Disloyal?

That New Consumers are potentially less loyal than Old has been confirmed by a swathe of recent surveys and studies. Research conducted by my own consultancy in the UK and USA suggests the following:

- One in five New Consumers feels little or no loyalty to any particular supplier and views every transaction on its own merits. More than two-thirds of Old Consumers express such loyalty.
- Two-thirds of New Consumers say they are always open to a better offer, compared to less than a third of Old Consumers.
- One in ten New Consumers regards those who remain loyal to a particular supplier as 'fools who fail to get the best possible deals', an opinion shared by less than one in thirty Old Consumers.
- Only one New Consumer in twenty insists that nothing would ever persuade them to leave a favored supplier, while among Old Consumers over half claim they would never do so.

From this it might appear that New Consumers are inherently and irredeemably disloyal, while Old Consumers are unquestioningly loyal. In fact, New Consumers have the potential to become far more loyal than the Old. The fact that they seldom are stems largely from companies being so delighted with their success in recruiting Old Consumers that they assume the same tactics will work with the New. Unfortunately, all they usually produce is pseudo loyalty and this, as they learn to their cost, can vanish as swiftly as the morning dew.

Authentic Loyalty vs Pseudo Loyalty

Loyalty consists of a primary response consisting of behavior and a secondary, emotional response involving affection for and feelings of attachment to the person, product or company concerned.

Pseudo loyalty consists of only the primary response, while authentic loyalty involves both a behavioral and an emotional element.

	Responses		
	Primary	**Secondary**	**Outcome**
Pseudo loyalty	Repeat business	Neutral	Short-term loyalty
Authentic loyalty	Repeat business	Positive	Long-term loyalty

The primary response of both pseudo and authentically loyal consumers is identical. Both allocate the manufacturer or service provider to whom they feel loyalty a greater share of their time, attention and income than they do to competitors.

Because the primary response involves a real and measurable benefit to the company, many settle for this and never attempt to develop a closer emotional bond. Because of this the consumer never becomes psychologically 'locked into' the relationship and is always open to a better offer.

As an example, consider the fate of the humble teabag. In the 1980s the brand leader in the £600 million tea market was PG Tips, which had been number one for more than 30 years. Its television commercials featured those persuasive chimps I described earlier. At number two, and seemingly destined to remain there, was Tetley's Tea, which had an equally long-running advertising campaign centered around cartoon characters known as the 'Tetley tea folk'. The loyalty of PG Tips drinkers had been established over such a long period that the company may have felt it could be taken for granted. Perhaps that might have been the case had not Tetley's introduced a small, but extremely costly innovation – the circular teabag. Within a year it had taken over as brand leader. 'One change was all it took to topple thirty-five years of what they would call loyalty,' comments John Grant, who once worked for PG Tips.

Another, no less serious hazard with pseudo loyalty is that because the consumer is not emotionally motivated, he or she is unlikely to become an advocate for the company by recommending it to friends and relatives.

Before looking at practical ways of encouraging New Consumers to become authentically loyal, we need to examine the six ways in which pseudo loyalty is generated.

Necessity

Shoppers in the former Soviet Union did not patronise retailers such as Moscow's GUM (State Department Store) because the 150 shops comprising Russia's largest department store offered the widest choices, highest quality and keenest prices. They did so because they had no alternative and, as soon as that necessity disappeared, so did most of the shoppers.

The local monopoly enjoyed by general stores in many small US towns prior to the Second World War resulted in similar 'loyalty' out of necessity. Retailers usually enjoyed the support of their community because there were so few convenient alternatives. The New Economy means that companies are no longer competing within national boundaries but in a global marketplace. As e-tailing and e-commerce become ever more firmly established and easy to access, this trend will play an even more significant role with customers surfing the net in search of the best deals going.

Personal liking

While necessity certainly plays an important role in the survival of many small, family-owned businesses, so too do the bonds of personal affection that often develop between suppliers and customers. In such cases customers are, of course, usually being loyal not to the business itself but to an individual within the company. In the past, where the same family sometimes served a community for generations, the proprietors were able to develop personal relationships with their customers. These neighborhood storekeepers knew all about the likes and dislikes of every single regular customer, as well as large chunks of their family history. As stores and communities grew larger and increasingly impersonal, these bonds of loyalty disappeared. On the rare occasions now when large organizations attract an admiring and affectionate following, it is usually only because they are headed by charismatic and well-known individuals.

Some 20 years ago when Freddie Laker's Skytrain was driven out of business, by what he claimed were the 'predatory and monopolistic' practices of other airlines, admirers around the world sent him donations, large and small, in a futile attempt to save his doomed airline.

Convenience

Since time and attention are the new scarcities, anything that enables New Consumers to save either of them will command 'loyalty' – right up to the moment that something even faster and more efficient comes along. High-street supermarkets offered greater convenience than smaller retailers, until out-of-town stores added ease of parking and greater choice to the package.

They too are coming under increasing threat from e-commerce, with orders placed over the internet for later delivery to the home or office. This is not to suggest that convenience plays no role in creating genuinely loyal customers; in many sectors it is an extremely important component. But there are two reasons that it can never be the whole story. Companies that base their appeal solely on offering greater convenience than their rivals will always be playing a game of catch-up. No sooner will one major retailer introduce an innovation designed to win loyalty by making its service more convenient than its rivals than others will either quickly do the same or attempt to deflect the attack in some way. No sooner will one retailer introduce new technology to make shopping at its stores slightly more convenient, for instance by offering personal barcode scanners so customers can bypass the checkout queues, than competitors will do the same.

Where New Consumers are concerned, convenience is a necessary but not sufficient condition for showing genuine loyalty.

Habit

People shop at certain stores, cheer along a particular football team or vote for a political party not out of any great intellectual or emotional conviction but simply because they have always done so. They do it because their friends and neighbors do it, because role models in the media and on TV do it, because their parents did it. Old Consumers are more likely to demonstrate this type of pseudo loyalty than New, due both to their being generally less well informed about alternative suppliers and because they feel more secure when following a well-trodden path than if they branch out on their own.

New Consumers, by contrast, are 'informationally empowered' and considerably more selective about where they spend their money. They can easily compare prices and research quality, they will discuss new products with one another, read product information and watch consumer programs on TV.

As Richard Oliver points out:

> *The day of the passive consumer has vanished. If not willingly provided with the full information they want, customers go elsewhere with little hesitation. With competitive product information just a keystroke away on the Internet, customer-switching costs are now near zero.*[1]

New Consumers are not only more involved in the processes of production and consumption, but their independent and individualistic approach to life causes them to avoid, whenever possible, the mass produced and mass-marketed goods and services that Old Consumers enjoy.

Bribery

Since 1997 when loyalty cards were first introduced in the UK by Tesco's, an estimated 90 million have been issued and 35 million are in regular use. Four out of ten American and six out of ten British shoppers possess at least one, with half owning two or more. The paradox is that because retailers are all racing to offer easily accessible loyalty schemes, there is little to distinguish between them.

A study that my consultancy conducted on behalf of ICL found that the mere possession of a loyalty card does necessarily encourage New Consumers to shop more frequently at a particular store. Seventy five percent of shoppers in the US and 70 per cent of those in the UK said that possessing a particular card did not encourage them to shop more often at the store concerned. Equally, four out of ten US and two out of ten UK shoppers admitted that they rarely made use of loyalty points or collected the rewards offered. Finally, ownership of a loyalty card ranks a long way down in the list of priorities when deciding which supermarket to patronise. Loyalty cards that are ill considered or poorly regulated can turn out to be an expensive mistake, either in terms of lost revenue, or bad publicity or both.

Even more obvious bribes intended to generate consumer loyalty are discounted prices and known value items (KVIs) sold at or below cost as loss leaders. Because the normal cost of KVIs is familiar to consumers, they can quickly and easily see how much they are saving. Unfortunately, as retailers know only too well, price cuts acclimatize customers to lower prices – when these return to normal, people switch to a cheaper brand.

Because cost is often less of a consideration for New Consumers than Old, lowering prices in an attempt to gain their loyalty could well prove counter-productive. As Mike Watkins, ACNielsen's manager of retail services, succinctly puts it: 'Discount shoppers in the UK are the most promiscuous of all shopper types.'

Lock-ins

If it costs a consumer more to switch than to stay, they are said to be locked in to that supplier. For example, if a company has invested a large amount of money in setting up a computer network and training staff, it may stay with that system even if it turns out to be less efficient than expected. Throwing it out and starting from scratch would be too expensive – in terms of outlay, downtime and, in many cases, corporate egos.

That said, some lock-ins turn out to be far less secure than anyone would have expected. It used to be believed, for example, that internet users were locked into their service provider because notifying scores, perhaps hundreds, of contacts that their e-mail address had been changed would prove so tedious and time consuming. In 1996, this belief was shattered after America Online developed a technical glitch resulting in a busy signal. Almost immediately, tens of thousands of supposedly locked-in customers moved to a different ISP.

As global competition builds to an intensity unseen in the history of commerce, companies will increasingly develop ways of breaking through the barriers created by loyalty lock-ins.

Locked in to a mobile phone network through a contractual arrangement or the need to keep the same number? A rival network will willingly sort out the problem in return for your custom.

Locked into credit card A by unpaid loans? Credit card B will take over that debt and even offer you a discount for joining it.

Whatever the lock-in, no matter how tightly bound a consumer and supplier may appear to be, someone, somewhere, will come up with a way of cutting them loose in exchange for locking them into their own system.

Given the elements of individuality, involvement and independence that characterize New Consumers, it is hardly surprising that lock-ins and mass-produced loyalty schemes hold little appeal for them. While they may well sign up to such programs and enjoy the benefits provided, even the best-run and most generous systems of discounts, reward points, air miles and upgrades are unlikely – on their own – to secure anything other than pseudo loyalty.

In many cases, only when New Consumers are able to perceive some measure of authenticity in the product or service on offer will they move from a primary to a secondary response, demonstrating not only genuine loyalty but actively encouraging others to follow their example. The only route to authentic loyalty, in an era where high quality and competitive prices are taken as givens, is to get the customer to genuinely like and trust your company.

Building Loyalty Online

In 1999, retail sales via the internet in the US, which amounted to less than 2 percent of total retail sales, still earned in excess of $6 billion. With the proportion of sales online predicted by some to reach 37 percent of total retail sales within 10 years, it is small wonder that companies are scrabbling to compete in this arena.

For pure play internet retailers, that is those without any high street presence, acquiring a new customer currently costs around $83 in advertising and marketing, according to a recent Shop.org and Boston Consulting Group report. The acquisition costs are somewhat lower for high street-based clicks-and-mortar companies, thanks to established brands and an existing customer base. Saks Fifth Avenue, for example, received thousands of hits on its new site even before the official launch. 'Brand loyalty in such a case is huge,' says Rohit Agarwal, vice-president of marketing at CommercialWare, a retail software solutions company.[2]

Even so, even already established retailers will be looking to spend in excess of $1.4 billion on advertising during the coming year. Given this level of cost, having won interest from a customer, retailers must make exceptional efforts to retain them.

Unfortunately, e-customers in the B2C (business to consumer) sector are notorious for being disloyal. Peter Burke, internet strategy director at Logobrand, comments:

> *The type of people online at the moment are flitters, channel-hoppers, who use the web to find the next lowest price and the next fastest delivery. And this conflicts with the loyalty package.*[3]

This inevitably raises the question of whether the loyalty of New Consumers can ever be ensured and, if so, how.

Some companies are following traditional marketing methods online. Coca-Cola, for example, linked up with internet auction house QXL.com to attract teenagers who are ineligible for credit cards. Customers collect ring pulls, which they convert into Coke credits that can then be used as currency to bid for goods online. QXL reported that up to 70,000 people can be bidding online at any one time and believes that the initiative added real value to its business.

Similarly, Virgin put its I-can loyalty scheme on the net, enabling consumers to obtain discounts off products in its portfolio, such as Virgin mobile phones for £30, 40 percent off books from Virgin Publishing and last-minute deals on Virgin holidays. It claims that sales of Virgin Cola have increased by 15 percent since the start of the scheme and that people are spending longer at the site, an average of seven minutes.

However, it seems highly doubtful that these methods will be successful in attracting genuine as opposed to pseudo loyalty online. Brian Blair, head of marketing for Europe at Modern Media, warns:

> *Building genuine loyalty online isn't about schemes or gimmicks ... In the digital world it's about providing a service that answers the customer's question: 'What can you do for me?' If you can't answer that question within a few seconds then customers will go elsewhere. We recognize that the customer is in complete control of a digital relationship and brand loyalty is a mouse click away. The individual has the power to dictate where he/she will go online, which allows individuals to dictate what brands will mean for them. So individual brands and their message will be tailored to individual needs.*[4]

A far better strategy is to take account of both the key scarcities that beset New Consumers, time and attention, while recognizing the tremendous importance they attach to being treated as individuals who not only want but demand to be seen as special. Such a strategy requires the following steps to be taken:

♦ Radically simplify the processes that customers use to buy products and services. Our research suggests that all too often, corporate amnesia sets in after the first order, with time-pressed customers being expected to explain all over again who they are, why they have contacted the service and how far they have progressed, together with any credit card details.

♦ Streamline business processes that link storefront, customer relationship management and resource planning systems. Retailers must make certain that the link between procurement and manufacturing is sufficient to deliver the goods to customers as rapidly and as cost-effectively as possible.

♦ Consolidate information regarding each customer's purchasing patterns with other business intelligence in order to identify their taste-space and be able to make highly targeted offers and suggestions. JC Penney, for example, uses proprietary technology that automatically enters its most loyal and valued customers into a privilege scheme, which recognizes them when they return to the site and gives them content based on their previous buying patterns.

♦ Create sites that go beyond merely advertising products and offer added interest and value. The Dove site, for instance, does not just give information about the soap brand but offers lifestyle-oriented features on such topics as relaxation techniques and other elements promoting a feel-good factor.

♦ Seek to build a personal relationship with the New Consumer through the site. Kristina Nordsten, principal consultant at PA Consulting, explains:

The world is so promiscuous and consumers have gone from shoppers to swappers within a certain repertoire. When you create conversations with customers online, it should be a strategically rich dialogue. You should suck customers in and make them become part of the content.[4]

While building loyalty online makes different technical demands on companies, the most crucial element for success remains the same –

generating loyalty by providing New Consumers with what they consider to be an authentic service. This is, in turn, achieved by ensuring that each customer feels not merely satisfied with the transaction but *super*satisfied.

Generating Authentic Loyalty through Supersatisfaction

The crucial distinction between satisfied and supersatisfied consumers was demonstrated more than a decade ago in a landmark study by the Xerox Corporation. It found that if satisfaction levels were measured on a scale of 1 (completely dissatisfied) to 5 (completely satisfied), those customers rating the service at 4 (satisfied) were six times more likely to be disloyal than those giving it the maximum of 5.

Before they will become authentically loyal, New Consumers must feel supersatisfied with what Tom Peters has described as the 'look and the feel and the smell and the taste' of doing business with a particular company. Authentic loyalty, then, can only be achieved by providing what I described in Chapter 1 as *miryokuteki hinshitsu*, quality that fascinates, rather than *atarimae hinshitsu*, quality that is expected.

Outcome and process dimensions

As we saw in Chapter 6, there are two aspects to the delivery of any product or service. The outcome dimension refers to the suitability and reliability of what is sold. Someone purchasing a holiday, for example, expects the travel agency to book tickets on the correct flights and reserve rooms in a hotel closely matching their brochure details. Suppliers will not supersatisfy New Consumers by meeting their expectations as to the outcome dimension – they will only arouse criticism by failing to do so.

The second aspect is the process dimension, or the manner in which a product or service is delivered. This has four components[6]:

◆ Tangibles – including everything that your customer sees, hears or touches. These include the appearance of company offices or showrooms, retail premises, reception and bedrooms and public areas in hotels, notepaper, brochures, sales literature, advertising and so on.

◆ Responsiveness – the speed with which customers' needs are satisfied and the willingness of staff to help.

◆ Assurance – the knowledge and expertise possessed by employees, their courtesy in addressing customer needs and the trust and confidence with which they communicate.

◆ Empathy – customers' belief that they are being listened to and understood by the supplier and that the attention they receive is genuinely caring and tailored to meet their specific needs.

While each of these is obviously important to every customer, the process dimension becomes even more crucial with New Consumers, whose overall expectations tend to be far higher and whose zone of tolerance is much narrower.

Tangibles matter because New Consumers expect every detail of an important transaction to be as perfect as possible. Responsiveness is important because they are frequently under intense time pressure themselves. Assurance and empathy are fundamental to the New Consumer's quest for authenticity. Synthetic service of the 'have a nice day' variety, often mouthed in a monotone and accompanied by a scowl, is regarded by most as an assault on their personal worth as an individual. It makes them feel like 'another faceless customer' when they desperately want to be regarded as special and different.

Judging outcome and service dimensions

The outcome dimension can, of course, only be assessed once the product or service has actually been delivered. You cannot know whether a car performs as specified or a ready prepared meal is tasty, for example, until you have driven one and eaten the other. New Consumers now take this dimension as a given and award few if any points for its attainment. Customers judge the process dimension as the service is being delivered. It is at this point, therefore, that an opportunity arises for building authentic loyalty among New Consumers.

A service or product delivered at below what the consumer regards as satisfactory places the manufacturer and supplier concerned at a competitive disadvantage. Its customers will have little or no loyalty and will move to a competitor without a moment's hesitation.

Companies that consistently satisfy their customers' expectations but do no more will still generate only pseudo loyalty, giving them a competitive advantage over those providing a poorer service but no guarantee of long-term loyalty.

Authentic loyalty can only be generated when companies consistently go *beyond* the consumers' best expectations and leave them feeling supersatisfied by the experience. These customers will not only be more likely to remain loyal but, in addition, become unpaid mavens, recommending the company to friends and colleagues.

Perhaps all this sounds like nothing more than common sense; certainly it should be. Yet in more than a decade of studying service standards in organizations ranging from supermarkets to corner shops, airlines to airports and hotels to hospitals, I have found few that came even close to consistently and reliably delivering a service resulting in supersatisfaction. In many cases, the empathy, assurance and responsiveness they displayed fell very far below this standard, even when the product they were selling was reliable and their tangibles were exemplary.

To enhance these process dimension, it is not normally necessary to spend large sums of money. All that is required is the training and incentives that will enable employees, at all levels within the organization, to deliver the very best standards of service of which they are capable.

Supersatisfaction and acts of spontaneous courtesy

In any type of business there exist 'moments of truth' – the points of delivery, the moments when company and consumer come face to face. This frequently happens away from supervision, when employees are on their own with the consumer. In these situations, they will only be capable of delivering on the promise of the brand if they regard its values as their own and not merely an edict imposed by management.

During these moments, customers may be exposed either to acts of spontaneous courtesy or, as more often happens, spontaneous discourtesy – remember the elderly woman shopper I described in Chapter 7.

When they occur, acts of spontaneous courtesy can transform the moment of truth from a mundane encounter into one quite capable of triggering authentic loyalty, not only in those at whom the action is directed but even to bystanders. Let me give you an example from my own experience. Not long ago I was traveling by rail from Gatwick airport to London. The train was crowded with holidaymakers, including a party of middle-aged American tourists, and airline staff. Among these were two uniformed British Airways stewards. Seeing that some of the Americans were having difficulty with their luggage and in finding seats, they immediately went to their assistance, sorting out the cases and ensuring that couples were able to sit together. It was an act of spontaneous courtesy, away from the workplace, that impressed other passengers as well as the tourists concerned.

Acts of spontaneous courtesy are one of the quickest, easiest and least costly ways of creating authentic loyalty among New Consumers, so they should be encouraged and rewarded in employees at all levels. Unfortunately, as a survey of 1000 employees by brand consultancy Siegel & Gale has shown, a majority of companies appear to make little or no effort to recruit the hearts and minds of their staff in this manner. Peter Gilson, the consultancy's managing director, explains:

> *We found the goals and objectives of different companies were well understood by outside parties through corporate brochures and annual reports, but not by people working at the coal-face. Yet the transfer of business strategy from the top to the bottom of the organization is critical, especially where lower-level employees are dealing with customers on a daily basis.*

The problem is more often one of faulty communications than a deliberate policy of keeping employees in the dark. Some companies, such as Virgin Atlantic, 3M, Apple and Motorola, have broken through the barrier and benefited from a focused and informed workforce. In any large organization it is the middle management level that must be given what Gilson terms 'the understanding and resources to drive the message through', since studies have shown that lower-level employees are more likely to trust them than those at a senior level.

Moments of truth may last only seconds, yet research has clearly shown that around 70 percent of customer satisfaction or dissatisfaction arises during this brief period. This is the moment when customer loyalty is born or blown.

Barriers to Supersatisfaction

From what I have said so far, it may appear that all a company need do in order to create authentically loyal New Consumers is to provide the highest possible level of service, all day and every day, around the clock and throughout the year. While this would certainly convince a significant number of consumers to become authentically loyal, my research suggests that even these paragons of virtue will still lose a significant proportion of New Consumers.

'We're used to thinking – assuming really – that satisfaction and loyalty move in tandem,' comments *Fortune* writer Thomas A. Stewart. 'The assumption's wrong.'[7]

There are three reasons for this being the case. First, exactly what comprises supersatisfaction is, to some extent, subjective. No matter how hard a company strives to excel, there will always be a proportion of customers who remain unimpressed. Perhaps when they tried it for the first time quality control systems failed and they received a service below that expected. This will inevitably occur from time to time and efficiently managed companies should, of course, have safety nets capable of catching and correcting these occasional mistakes. It could also be that expectations were unrealistically high, so that no matter what you did to please them they would still feel aggrieved.

Similarly, a product or service that some New Consumers regard as possessing a quality that fascinates may strike others as mundane. Finally, as New Consumers become accustomed to a certain level of service or quality of product, they start taking this as their baseline expectation and demand even better service or quality in order to feel supersatisfied.

Building Authentic Loyalty on a Basis of Authenticity

Given the elements of individuality, involvement and independence that characterize New Consumers, they will shift from pseudo to authentic loyalty and actively encourage others to follow their example only if they are able to perceive some measure of authenticity in the product

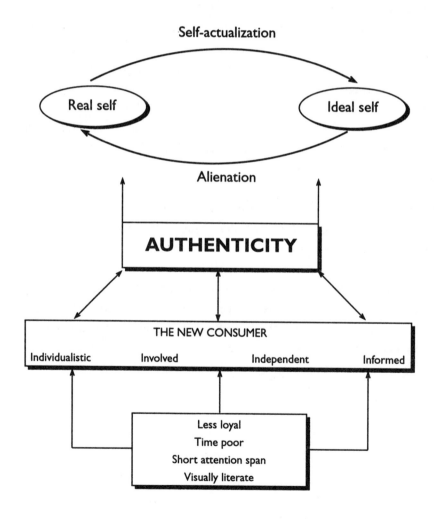

193

or service on offer. A product or service that is considered authentic is, almost by definition, one that can be trusted to do what is claimed for it. By allocating some of their scarce resources of trust to authentic products and services, therefore, New Consumers save themselves more of the equally scarce time and attention needed to find and test out alternatives.

One cannot mass produce authenticity. Rather, it has to be introduced on an almost person-to-person basis, with individual needs, desires, expectations and interests being fully accounted for. Until fairly recently, such a task would have been beyond all but the smallest supplier, the corner-shop retailer, a specialist workshop or individual craftspeople who could get to know the tastes and needs of their limited customer base at a personal level. Today, computer analysis of consumer information enables companies to create an intimate tastespace chart of each individual customer's preferences. This allows even the largest company to offer the 'personal service approach' that many New Consumers regard as authentic. As business analyst Fredrick F. Reichheld comments:

> *Doing business with people you trust and understand is more predictable and efficient, and thus more profitable, than doing business with uninvested strangers.*[8]

Providing an authentic product or service and then delivering it in an equally authentic manner is not only the way to ensure authentically loyal consumers, but also the fastest route to commercial success in the New Economy.

Summary

◆ What many suppliers regard as loyalty on the part of their customers is often only partial and temporary pseudo loyalty.

◆ Companies with pseudo-loyal customers are vulnerable to high levels of customer turnover whenever competitors make more attractive offers.

◆ Loyalty is made up of two responses, a primary one comprising behavior and a secondary one involving positive emotions towards the product or service. Only when both are present can the consumer be considered authentically loyal.

◆ Although they have a high potential to be disloyal, we believe New Consumers can also be transformed into the most authentically loyal customers any supplier could hope to find.

◆ Authentically loyal consumers are not only dedicated to a particular supplier, but prepared to act as unpaid advocates or mavens for that company.

◆ Creating authentic loyalty involves providing an authentic product or service in a manner that New Consumers also regard as authentic.

10

Giving the Soul Control

People have always striven to control the events that affect their lives. By exerting influence in the spheres over which they can command some control, they are better able to realize desired futures and to forestall undesired ones.

Albert Bandura, Self-Efficacy: The Exercise of Control

Damocles, a courtier to Dionysius the Elder of Syracuse, was a world-class sycophant. While it was only prudent to keep a civil tongue in your head if you wanted to keep your head at all at the tyrant's court, Damocles was so obsequious that even the emperor finally grew tired of his outrageous flattery.

One night Dionysius invited Damocles to a sumptuous banquet and placed him on the royal throne. The courtier's delight at this honor rapidly changed to terror, however, when he saw a naked sword, suspended by a single hair, hanging directly over his head.

The emperor's purpose was to demonstrate to Damocles the crucial distinction between power and control. As a tyrant, Dionysius enjoyed absolute authority over his subjects, yet being mortal he had no more control over his destiny than the wretched courtier. Both were no more than a hair's breadth from disaster.

This ancient story – dating from around the third century BC – is highly relevant in understanding exactly what it is that New Consumers really want from suppliers.

For at least two decades companies large and small have been striving to persuade consumers of their belief that the 'customer is king' in the expectation that, by doing so, competitive success will be assured. This philosophy of empowerment received early and enthusiastic endorsement from Tom Peters and Robert Waterman: 'The best companies are pushed around by their customers, and they love it,' they noted approvingly in their 1982 bestselling classic, *In Search of Excellence*. 'The user is supreme as a generator and tester of ideas.'

As we saw in Chapter 9, while treating customers with courtesy and consideration is a precondition for commercial success it is not, in itself, a sufficient condition. All the consumer benefits implicit in such 'customer is king' strategies as 'relationship marketing,' 'one to one selling' and 'putting the customer first' are *taken for granted* by New Consumers. As a consequence, delivering on such promises provides little if any competitive advantage – although failure to do so certainly places that company at a significant disadvantage compared to more customer-oriented concerns.

Because they take good service for granted and are looking for other benefits, independent-minded New Consumers are autonomous in their purchasing decisions. Although this demands more time and attention than following the herd and buying what everyone else is buying, it remains the most viable strategy at times of social change when the market is fragmenting into smaller and smaller self-interest groups.

Unfortunately, such a stance also leads to greater levels of uncertainty and stress, since by adopting an independent position one automatically loses the comfort blanket that comes from knowing that millions of others are thinking and behaving in exactly the same way. The isolation that results from being inwardly directed accounts for the feelings of alienation from the mainstream of society experienced by significant numbers of New Consumers.

Martin Hayward, of the UK-based Henley Centre, explains:

Society is now incredibly fluid. Today's consumers are better off but more confused and less predictable than ever before. With so many choices and opportunities, they can now decide to a far greater extent who and what they are.[1]

The antidote to such alienation is to feel in control of situations. The greater our sense of control, the less stress we will experience even when we are acting independently. While New Consumers are no less acquisitive than the Old they are, as we have seen, far more motivated by their quest for authenticity.

In his book *Spiritual Marketplace*, Wade Clark Roof says of this search for personally meaningful truth:

The energizing forces arise out of quests not so much for group identity or social location as for an authentic inner life.

As I explained in Chapter 2, New Consumers frequently see the acquisition of authentic products and services as a means of achieving self-actualization, the peak of Abraham Maslow's hierarchy of needs, signaling the attainment of our true potential. Such an accomplishment holds out the tantalizing possibility of extending control over every aspect of our psychological life, over thoughts and emotions, actions and reactions, self-confidence and self-esteem.

Control in Commercial Transactions

Control in this context means ensuring that the small details, as well the main aspects, of any transaction are dealt with efficiently. Imagine, for example, telephoning a new supplier with whom you are considering placing an order. Your call is put through to a call center, and you have to press a succession of buttons to get through to the department you want. You are then held in a queue and played irritating music, while being interrupted every few seconds by a computerized voice telling you that your call is important to the company and you will be answered shortly. Worse still, you are told that all the operators are busy and asked to call back; if you hold, you are told 'goodbye' in a very firm voice and then cut off.

When you finally do get through, the company is out of stock of the product you want and offers a substitute, but is unable to quote on delivery. The person promises to phone you back with an exact date but fails to do so.

At each stage of the process, the company – or a machine – rather than the customer has been controlling the outcomes. For any potential customers such a response would be frustrating and alienating; for New Consumers in an era of abundance and choice it is likely to end all further contact. They want to be in control, and they want to be in control now.

Giving Control to New Consumers

What can manufacturers, suppliers and retailers do to ensure that New Consumers feel in control of every aspect of the transaction, from the first approach to delivery of the product or service? There are five key issues to be borne in mind if a company is to meet the needs of New Consumers by giving their souls control.

Understand tastespace

As I explained in Chapter 4, tastespace can be understood either through personal knowledge of the individual or, as is far more likely, though extensive and detailed analysis of their previous purchases.

Marketing to consumers by treating them as averages of anything will increasingly prove counter-productive. As mathematician John Allen Paulos comments in his immensely entertaining book *Once Upon a Number*:

> *Even when they are true, to take an extreme example, there is something inhuman and vaguely pornographic about statistics that maintain that since half the people in the United States are men and half are women, the average American adult has one ovary*

> *and one testicle. Or that the average resident of Dade County, Florida, is born Hispanic and dies Jewish.*

Not only will New Consumers who consider themselves marketed to *en masse* be more likely to reject than accept that particular offer, they will also be far less prepared to extend further time, attention or trust to the company. In the New Economy you will find only two kinds of business – the very quick and the very dead.

Add authenticity and win trust

As the speed with which new and original products are transformed into commodities reduces, those that can most easily be reproduced rapidly fall in value, while those with genuinely authentic features hold or even increase their worth.

Increasing choice combined with New Consumers' high expectations of quality make the addition of authenticity essential if your particular product or service is to stand out in an ever more crowded and competitive marketplace.

As I explained in Chapter 2, there are four main routes by which authenticity can be attached to a product or service. Originality and credibility are important, as is locating the offering in a specific place or particular moment of time.

As well as establishing authenticity, it is important to gain New Consumers' trust. Some companies seek to establish trust by means of a charismatic and eloquent spokesperson who is usually, though not necessarily, the company's founder.

It is not necessary to have first-rank celebrity status in order to be seen as a reliable and honest person with whom to do business. Johnnie Boden, founder of Boden, a $24 million a year turnover mail-order clothes company, is hardly a household name. Yet he has still been able to use his open and friendly personality to build an intensely loyal following. Johnnie's business has prospered because his customers feel they know him as an individual. They recognize him in the street and stop to chat about the latest garments, they buttonhole him in restaurants to offer congratulations on a new line and, above all, they trust him. They also feel that he has personal authenticity, making him and his company doubly attractive to the New Consumer.

The downside, as I have already explained, if that if ever these leaders fall from grace, they can throw into doubt the credibility of the whole company.

The second method for gaining trust is through creating a space of safety, a third place that is neither home nor work but in which people feel secure, as I described in Chapter 6. In such a refuge from the world or in its virtual equivalent of cyberspace communities, New Consumers are able to meet up with friends or make new ones, exchange ideas, swap gossip, pass on news and generally chill out.

Respect scarcities of time and attention

When, like the wedding guest in Coleridge's *Ancient Mariner*, New Consumers 'cannot choose but hear', their annoyance and frustration are most likely to result in the message being rejected outright.

Even when permission has been obtained, only the absolute minimum of time and attention should be expected. When selling via the internet, for example, websites must be easy to find and rapid to use, without any complex graphics that take too much time to download, or difficult-to-navigate options that make excessive demands on both time and attention. Service in the virtual world must also be at least equal to that received when the customer is visiting a physical business – an important point seemingly ignored by many companies, as evidenced by US research indicating that 24 percent of websites surveyed did not provide pre-sales assistance, 32 percent gave no purchase instructions, and on only 20 percent of sites was there information on product availability.

While New Consumers are prepared to invest in anything they find both personally relevant and rewarding, they will not readily forgive companies that hijack or squander their scarce resources. This is, of course, exactly what happens with television commercials that interrupt their favourite programs, telling them things that are frequently irrelevant to their lives, and, even when relevant, of little interest. To combat this they may leave the room or change channels, often not so much because these are more rewarding alternatives but in order to feel they are back in control of events.

For companies to succeed in getting their message across to these impatient New Consumers, their investments of time and attention must be rewarded. One way with television commercials is to make them so entertaining that audiences *choose* to view them. Another route that some advertisers are adopting is to pay internet users, either in cash or in kind, to read their messages.

But it is not just in marketing their products or services that companies must keep the New Consumer's scarcities of time and attention firmly in mind. The same applies to every aspect of the transaction, from making contact with your organization in the first place by having an easy-to-remember telephone number or web address, to the instructions that accompany the product or service. They must be borne in mind when setting up helplines and advice desks, both in the ease with which these can be contacted and the clarity of the information they provide. Don't expect a New Consumer to wait days for a response to an email, for example.

Review your procedures with the scarcities of time and attention in mind and you are almost certain to find room for improvement. Even if your whole life revolves around the production of widgets, for the most part the outside world will view them with the greatest indifference. See the marketplace through the eyes of the New Consumer and the way you seek to do business with them will start to look very different.

Involve them

Transport yourself for a moment to an open-air market in France, Italy or Spain. Imagine you are part of the crowds jostling around every stall, smelling the aromas of fresh fruit, vegetables, flowers, cheeses, coffee, freshly baked bread and smoked meats. Look at the heaps of produce, the piles of pastries, the iced slabs of fish. Test the fruit for ripeness, select the most appetizing cuts of meat, the choicest vegetables. Your senses are bombarded by the sights and sounds of the market. It is an environment in which even the most mundane domestic shopping becomes a treat and an adventure rather than an often stressful and mostly tedious chore.

This same sense of involvement is what New Consumers are seeking when out shopping, especially for impulse purchases, and it is by giving them such hands-on experiences that companies such as cosmetics retailer Lush have become so successful. The retail environment should draw people in and encourage them to handle the merchandise, rather than create barriers between consumers and what is there to be consumed.

In 1998, for example, Estée Lauder increased sales by almost a quarter when it replaced traditional glass counters with open displays and encouraged customers to handle the cosmetics, test out different products and browse freely without having to seek help.

Making it as easy as possible for New Consumers to handle, experiment with and test out your products, while immersing themselves in a warm, friendly and welcoming environment, will prove increasingly essential over the coming years. Stores of any kind that appear intimidating and more reminiscent of a museum than a marketplace are doomed to disappear.

Consumers as Producers

Kevin Kelly describes an analogy in the form of a puzzle posed by Stuart Brand:

> *In a 21st-Century society wired into instantaneous networks, marketing is the mirror; the collective consumer is the chameleon. What color is the consumer when you put him on the marketplace?*

This is a question that goes to the heart of understanding what New Consumers will buy and why in the New Economy, and one that also helps explain the frenetic rate at which so many authentic products are transformed into run-of-the-mill commodities.

To put the same analogy into a different context, imagine a new restaurant. Although it looks attractive and the food is excellent, initially only a few people choose to eat there. Other potential diners, walking past and seeing only a few tables occupied, continue on their way because most of us avoid almost empty restaurants. As more people start to come others are attracted in because the place is almost full and clearly popular. Eventually, however, the restaurant becomes so popular that congestion and difficulties in booking a table start putting people off and the number of diners once again declines. As the number of diners falls, people flock back since seats are now more readily available…

This oscillating model of supply and demand works fairly well so far as Old Consumers are concerned since, as we have seen, many of their consumption choices are determined by convenience and conformity. New Consumers, however, tend to move elsewhere as soon as something – a restaurant, a holiday resort or a product – becomes popular, as at this point it is seen to lose authenticity and revert to a commodity. Hence the closure of once fashionable restaurants and the abandonment of previously exclusive and favored resorts.

As chameleons, therefore, New Consumers choose one color and then change again when too many others start making the same choice.

Cool hunters, mavens and early adopting New Consumers are the first to show an interest in anything new. If the buzz they generate causes the product or service to become more widely known, more and more New Consumers will flock to take it up, until – unless suppliers take steps to prevent this from happening – authenticity is lost and New Consumers move away in search of something new and original.

The rate at which the authenticity–commodity cycle occurs depends on the network through which information is communicated. In the past this might have been via word of mouth, print media, cinema, radio and television.

As the New Economy increasingly connects these previously disparate channels of information into digital networks, the speed at which information can be produced and disseminated rises significantly. Together these networks will influence the desires and demands of New

Consumers to an even greater extent than radio and television captured the hearts and minds of the Old Consumers.

For example, there are over 100,000 participants in the Zagat Surveys of restaurants in more than 40 US and foreign cities, described by their originators as 'the "organized word-of-mouth" of sophisticated consumers'.[3] Each entry is given a rating based on the average of hundreds or even thousands of experiences.

As ever more readily available sources of real-time information start beaming back images of our own consuming behaviors, the activities of even a small group of New Consumers can exert a profound influence over the marketplace as a whole. Kevin Kelly puts it thus:

The modern world is being paved with mirrors. We have ubiquitous TV cameras, and ceaseless daily polling ('63 Percent of Us Are Divorced') to mirror back to us every nuance of our collective action ... Every consumer becomes both a reflector, a cause and an effect.[4]

With New Consumers and producers becoming increasingly enmeshed, differences between the two grow less and less distinct. Take, for example, the establishment of electronic standards, such as the CD, minidisk or DVD, in which consumer expectations of how other consumers will respond is crucial in determining which products will succeed and which will fail. Carl Shapiro and Hal Varian comment:

In competing to become the standard, or at least to achieve critical mass, consumer expectations are critical. In a very real sense, the product that is expected to become the standard will become the standard. Self-fulfilling expectations are one manifestation of positive-feedback economics and bandwagon effects. As a result, companies participating in markets with strong network effects seek to convince customers that their products will ultimately become the standard, while rival, incompatible products will soon be orphaned.

This is one reason for the growth in online auctions, which operate between consumers with no producer guiding choice in between.

New Consumers, with their basic necessities easily catered for, are free to focus on innovation, originality and authenticity – all of which, essentially, represent different aspects of information. And since one can never run out of information, the more that is consumed the more there is to consume. Thus consumption begets more consumption until it becomes both a compulsion and a way of life.

The Soul Is the Marketplace – the Marketplace Is the Soul

In a hypercompetitive world of fragmented markets and independently minded, well-informed individuals, companies that fail to understand and attend to the needs of New Consumers are doomed to extinction. The marketplace will be divided up between very large and extremely powerful corporations on the one hand and small, flexible, highly adaptable companies serving specialist niches on the other.

There will be little future in the New Economy for any business that is only moderately viable. Currently, the average life of a major company only rarely exceeds 40 years. In the coming decade, any business that is less than highly successful will find that lifespan reduced by a factor of at least ten.

The secret of commercial success in the New Economy lies in possessing a finely honed awareness of what these well-informed consumers will buy and why. In showing respect for their scarcities of time and attention and in assisting in their quest for authenticity. In recognizing their independent-minded individualism and in becoming deserving of their continued trust. In short, in understanding the soul of the New Consumer.

Appendix

The Mind Scan
Research Program

Starting in the late 1980s with experiments conducted at the University of Sussex, researchers from my consultancy have been measuring the electrical activity of the brain while subjects watch television commercials. The purpose of these studies was to determine whether such measures offer a helpful research tool in the study of viewer responses.

Such an approach is by no means new. In 1986, for example, researchers at the University of Wisconsin's School of Business published a paper entitled 'EEG activity and the processing of television commercials'.

The novelty of our work lies in the simplicity of the data obtained and the ease with which it can be converted to a graph that demands no specialist skills to interpret. One of the main problems with the early studies, which used medical EEG equipment to obtain their recordings, was the sheer volume of data produced during even a 30-second commercial.

The benefit of our equipment, which we developed especially for this research, is that the flow of data is held within manageable proportions without significant loss of vital information.

How Mind Scan Works

The Mind Scan system comprises a specialized electro encephalograph (EEG) together with a computer interface that detects, measures, records and analyzes electrical patterns in the left and right sides of the viewer's brain.

After filtering out the frequencies of interest to us, Mind Scan transforms the data into units of power per frequency range per period of time. While this may sound complicated, all it really means is that the information it provides is easily understood. It also allows us to combine brain output over a period of time. When analyzing commercials, we select time frames that correspond to the length of individual scenes. This permits the impact of each scene, together with its relationship to those that precede or follow it, to be evaluated and compared.

The only constraint is that the minimum period of time is large enough to enable the lower frequencies to be adequately observed. For alpha waves (see below) this is around one second.

Before describing some of the results obtained, we should explain a little about why such measures are of value, especially in distinguishing between the responses of New and Old Consumers.

Our Electric Brains

The brain may be likened to an electrically powered computer running at about eight watts. This electrical activity can be detected as 'brain waves' whose frequency (cycles per second) and power (amplitude) are continually varying depending on mental state and the intellectual challenges being faced.

Brain waves have been classified into a number of bands according to their frequency measured in Hertz (Hz). These bands are shown in the table opposite.

Of these, the two of interest to our research are alpha and beta waves.

Frequency of brain waves (Hz)	Name of brain state	Characteristics
0.5–4	Delta	Deeper states of sleep
4–8	Theta	Drowsiness, some dreaming Twilight sleep
8–14	Alpha	Relaxed wakefulness. Brain not engaged in any specific mental or emotional activity.
14–22	Beta	Alert behavior, concentrated mental activity. Also present when anxious and apprehensive
22–23	High beta	Increased anxiety or hyper responses and thinking
33+	K-complex and unnamed	Brief bursts during problem solving and memorizing

High alpha has been shown to be associated with a relaxed and hence not an especially attentive frame of mind. However, our research suggests that alpha output is more usefully considered in relation to beta wave production, since analyzing alpha output on its own gives a distorted impression of viewer response.

High beta combined with high alpha, for example, means that the viewer is not only paying attention to the commercial but is doing so in a relaxed, yet alert, frame of mind. However, when a pattern of falling beta and rising alpha is found, one can safely conclude that the subject is disinterested.

Beta waves, which are the second most common type produced by the human brain, provide a measure of attention and interest. For this reason, and for convenience in understanding responses to commercials, we have defined total beta output as the Index of Cortical Response (ICR). We consider this to provide a direct measure of how interested and attentive the viewer is to the commercial.

Left–Right Brain Differences

Research suggests that, for a right-handed person, the left side of the brain is more likely to be involved in logical, objective analysis while the right side is concerned with fantasy and imagination. In one study, artists were found to produce greater right-brain activity while accountants showed more left-brain dominance.

It seems likely, therefore, that during the episodic processing of an image-focused commercial there will be somewhat greater right-side activity.

Left-brain activity is more often associated with an intellectual approach to the commercial, while stronger right-brain activity indicates a more intuitive response. When a commercial is being processed on the basis of the factual information it contains, one tends to see greater activity on the left side of the brain in right-handed viewers (around 80 percent of the population).

It must always be remembered, however, that except in rare cases of severe damage, the human brain functions as a unified whole. It is as misleading to emphasize the importance of one hemisphere over the other in certain types of mental activity as it would be to suggest that the heart's left chambers are more essential than the right during physical exertion.

As Harvard cognitive psychologist Howard Gardner puts it:

Claims about the division of labor between its two halves are becoming increasingly remote from what is known or even suspected. Indeed, the current packaging of human-brain research threatens to reveal more about academic huckstering than about neurological function.

Notes

Preface to the Paperback Edition

1 'Grim prospects', *New Scientist*, 2 December 2000: 5
2 Mark Fischetti, *Scientific American*, November 2000: 33.

Chapter 1

1 Cited in Vance Packard, 1978: 128.
2 Personal communication to the author.
3 Bryan Appleyard, 'Essay', *Sunday Times Magazine*, 7 January 1999: 36–41.
4 From an interview with James Dyson by David Cheal published in *How to Spend It*.
5 This research was originally published in H.M. Guetzkow, *Groups, Leadership and Men*, in a paper entitled 'Effects of group pressure upon the modification and distortion of judgement'. When its replication was attempted in 1981, by Perrin and Spencer, they found very low rates of conformity. An alternative explanation for later students' refusal to go along with the obviously incorrect view of their peers is that when they wanted to replicate the experiment, psychologists were hard pressed to find any students who were not already aware of the original findings. The only departments in which naïve participants could be found were mathematics, chemistry and engineering. Such students may know nothing about psychology and care even less, but their scientific background may make them far

more likely to insist that their observations are accurate, no matter how many other people try to tell them differently!

6   Quoted in Lucia van der Post, 'How to stay a cuff above the rest', *Financial Times*, 9 August 1999.

7   'The e-corporation', *Fortune*, 8 December 1998.

Chapter 2

1   Cited in chapter 18 of Mark Pendergrast's fascinating *Uncommon Grounds: the History of Coffee and How it Transformed Our World*.

2   Vijay Vishwanath and David Harding, *Harvard Business Review*, March–April 2000: 17–18.

3   Cited in John Grant, *The New Marketing Manifesto*.

4   Jeremy Hunt, 'Race to put Titanic back to sea', *Sunday Business*, 24 October 1999: 9.

5   For an interesting exploration of Allport and his influence on modern psychology, see Morton Hunt's *The Story of Psychology*, pages 316–18.

6   Quoted from Maslow's *Towards a Psychology of Being*.

7   Cited in *The Fourth Discontinuity*.

8   David Corten cited in *When Corporations Ruled the World*.

9   Cited in Paul Lukas, 'Tippecanoe and Tylenol Too', *Fortune*, February 11999: 20.

10 Ohanian, 1991.

11 Malcolm Gladwell, 'Message in a bottle', *The Independent on Sunday Magazine*: 6.

12 Michael J. Wolf, 'The future of digital entertainment', *Scientific American*, November 2000: 33.

Chapter 3

1   'Dying for information', a report published by Reuters Business Information in 1996, was based on 1300 managers in the UK, US,

Singapore, Hong Kong and Australia.

2   Cited in Richard Saul Wurman's *Information Anxiety*.
3   *Methods for Satisfying the Needs of the Scientist and the Engineer for Scientific and Technical Communication*.
4   Michael de Kare Silver, 1999.
5   'Ads with legs and the writing on the wall', *Sunday Business*, 23 May 1999.
6   Theodore Levitt, 1960.
7   Janet Bush, 'Sting in the tail for new breed of bargain hunters', *The Times*, 11th November 1998: 33.

Chapter 4

1   *Business Week*, 26 January 1998.
2   'Market segmentation really is cool', *Market Leader*, Spring 1998.
3   Rachel Kennedy and Andrew Ehrenberg, 'What's in a brand?', *Research*, April 2000, Issue 407.
4   *Admap*, September 1993: 5
5   Keith McNamara, ICL internal white paper, 1998.
6   Cited in Mark Nicholson, 'Getting more value from the customers', *Financial Times*, 13 October 1999: 32.
7   John Hagel III and Jeffrey F. Rayport, 'The coming battle for customer information,' *Harvard Business Review*, January–February 1997: 55–67.
8   Nigel Morris, 'A truly intelligent customer', *Real Business*, June 1999: 66.
9   *Ibid.*

Chapter 5

1   Malcolm Gladwell, 1997: 86.
2   *Ibid.*: 84.
3   Naoko Nakamae, '"Girl power" helps Japan's retailers buck reces-

sion', *Financial Times*, 19 June 1999.

4 Richard Adams and Alice Rawsthorn, 'Renaissance of the cardigan helps shape vital statistics', *Financial Times*, 24 March 1999.

5 Gregory Schmid, 'Deregulating for the sophisticated consumer', white paper for the Institute for the Future (www.iftf.org).

6 Faith Popcorn with Lys Marigold (1996) *Clicking*, London: Thorsons: 282.

7 Cited by Quentin Curtis in 'Black magic', *Daily Telegraph Magazine*, October 1999: 58–62.

8 Kerry Capell, Larry Light & Ann Therese Palmer, 'Just wild about Harry', *Business Week*, 16 August 1999.

9 Gary Hamel & Jeff Sampler. (1998) 'The e-corporation', *Fortune*, 8 December: 52–63.

10 Quoted in Jones, 'Hey, yeah, get a life, mum', *The Bookseller*, 1999.

Chapter 6

1 Larry O'Brien & Frank Harris, 1991.
2 Michael Wolf, 1999: 77.
3 *Publishers Weekly*, 26 April 1999: 36.
4 Richard Dean, 'Let 'er rip', *Wired*, April 1999: 157.
5 Chuck Martin, 1997: 33.
6 Ken Irons, 1998.

Chapter 7

1 Mica Nava, 'Modernity's disavowal', in Pasi Falk & Colin Campbell, 1997: 66.

2 Peter Cochrane (1999) *Tips for Time Travelers*, New York: McGraw-Hill.

3 Irving Janis (1977), cited in 'Decision making under stress', in L. Goldberger and S. Breznitz (eds) 1982.

4 Larry Hochman, quoted in 'Into the unknown', *Tempus*, 15: 8.

Chapter 8

1 Jon Rees, 'Award-winning ads fail to sell', *Sunday Business*, 27 August 1999: 13.
2 *Ibid.*
3 John Caldwell, 1954: 5.
4 C. Bridgewater & A. Biel (1990) 'Television commercials', *Advertising Research*, June/July: 20.
5 Andrew Ehrenberg, professor of marketing at London's South Bank University, quoted in Richard Tomkins, 'Commercial breakdown', Financial Times, 5 August 1999: 19.
6 *Ibid.*
7 Graham Lancaster, 'Creating Time for Research', *Marketing*, 6 August 1992.
8 Betty Liu, 'Latin stars pops up at PepsiCo.', *Financial Time*, 3 September 1999.
9 Quoted in Carol Midgley, 'Elderly "almost extinct" on TV', *Time*, 8 September 1999: 4.
10 Quoted in Rees, *op. cit.*
11 Cited in Jon Rees, 'The name is Bond...James Bond. Licensed to fill the order books', *Sunday Business*, 14 March 1999: 13.
12 Quoted in John Williams, 'Scotching old perceptions', *Financial Times*, 19 November 1999: 16.

Chapter 9

1 Richard Oliver, 1999: 57.
2 Jennifer Saba, 'The costliest customers', *Business 2.0*, November 2000: 81.
3 'Netting loyalty', *Grocer*, 7 October 2000: 38–9.
4 *Ibid.*
5 *Ibid.*
6 A. Passamuran, A. Berry & L.L. Zeithaml (1991) 'Understanding customer expectations of service', *Sloan Management Review*, 32(3,

Spring): 39–48.

7 Thomas A Stewart, 'A satisfied customer isn't enough', *Fortune*, 21 July 1999: 70.

8 Frederick F. Reichheld, 1996: 2.

Chapter 10

1 Martin Hayward, Henley Centre, quoted in Stuart Wavell, 'Invasion of the mutant spenders', *The Sunday Times*, 22 November 1998.

2 Kevin Kelly, 1995: 90.

3 http://zagat.com/about/history.asp.

4 Kevin Kelly, *op.cit.*: 93.

Bibliography

Aaker, D.A. & Stayman, D.M. (1990) 'Measuring audience perception of commercials and relating them to ad. impact', *Journal of Advertising Research*, 30(4): 7–17.

Aaker, D.A. & Biel., A.L. (1993) *Brand Equity and Advertising: Advertising's Role in Building Strong Brands*, Hillsdale, NJ: Lawrence Erlbaum Associates.

Adams, S. (1998) *I'm Not Anti-Business, I'm Anti-Idiot: a Dilbert Book*, London: Boxtree.

Allport, G. (1971) *Personality*, London: Constable.

Anschuetz, N. (1997) 'Point of view: building brand popularity. The myth of segmenting to brand success', *Journal of Advertising Research*, 37(1): 63–6.

Aylott, R.M. & Mitchell,V.W. (1998) 'An exploratory study of grocery shopping stressors', *International Journal of Retail and Dustribution Management*, 26(9): 362–73.

Bakan, D. (1966) 'Behaviourism and American urbanization', *Journal of Historical and Behavioural Sciences*, (2): 5–28.

Baldinger, A.L.R. & Rubinson, J. (1996) 'Brand loyalty: the link between attitude and behaviour', *Journal of Advertising Research*, 36(6): 22–34.

Bandura, A. (1997) *Self-Efficacy: the Exercise of Control*, New York: W.H. Freeman.

Barnet, R. & Cavanagh, J. (1994) *Global Dreams*, New York: Simon and Schuster.

Bauman, Z. (1992) *Intimations of Postmodernity*, London: Routledge.

Baumeister, R.F. (1986) *Identity: Cultural Change and the Struggle for Self*, Oxford: Oxford University Press.

Bayley, S. (1991) *Taste: the Secret Meaning of Things*, London: Faber and Faber.

Bayton, J.A. (1958) 'Motivation, cognition, learning – basic factors in consumer behaviour', *Journal of Marketing*, 22: 282–9.

Bazin, A. (1967) *What Is Cinema?* Los Angeles, CA: University of California Press.

Beaujeu-Garnier, J. & Delobez, A. (1979) *Geography of Marketing*, London: Longman.

Bell, D. (1973) *The Coming of Post-Industrial Society: a Venture in Social Forecasting*, New York: Basic Books.

Bell, D. (1980) *The Social Framework of the Information Society*, Oxford: Blackwell.

Benson, J. (1994) *The Rise of Consumer Society in Britain: 1880–1980*, London & New York: Longman.

Berger, P. L. & Luckmann, T. (1967) *The Social Construction of Reality: a Treatise in the Sociology of Knowledge*, Harmondsworth: Penguin.

Biel, A.L. & Bridgewater, C.A. (1990) 'Attributes of likable television commercials', *Journal of Advertising Research*, (June–July): 38–43.

Bier, W.C. (ed.) (1972) *Alienation: Plight of Modern Man?*, New York: Fordham University Press.

Blair, M.H. (1988) 'An empirical investigation of advertising wearin and wearout', *Journal of Advertising Research*, (Dec/Jan): 45–50.

Blythman, J. (1996) *The Food We Eat*, London: Michael Joseph.

Bolter, D. (1984) *Turing's Man: Western Culture in the Computer Age*, London: Duckworth.

Bowlby, R. (1993) *Shopping with Freud*, London: Routledge.

Bowler, P.J. (1989) *The Invention of Progress: the Victorians and the Past*, Oxford: Basil Blackwell.

Bradley, S.P., Hausman, J.A. & Nolan, R.R. (1993) *Globalization, Technology and Competition: the Fusion of Computers and Telecommunications in the 1990s*, Boston, MA: Harvard Business School Press.

Branson, R. (1999) *Losing my Virginity: the Autobiography*, London: Virgin Publishing.

Branthwaite, A.S., *Capturing the Complexity of Advertising Perceptions*, Millward Brown International: 19.

Britt, S.H. (1966) *Consumer Behaviour and the Behavioural Sciences: Theories and Applications*, New York, John Wiley.

Britt, S.H. (1970) *Psychological Experiments in Consumer Behaviour*, New York: John Wiley.

Brothers, L.M.D. (1997) *Friday's Footprint: How Society Shapes the Human Mind*, New York/Oxford: Oxford University Press.

Brown, J.A.C. (1963) *Techniques of Persuasion: From Propaganda to Brainwashing*, Harmondsworth: Penguin.

Brown, K. (1999) 'Approval of big business in Britain at 30-year low', *Financial Times.* 1.

Brown, M. (1998) *The Spiritual Tourist*, London: Bloomsbury.

Budd, M., Craig, S. & Steinman, C. (1999) *Consuming Environments: Television and Commercial Culture*, New Jersey/London: Rutgers University Press.

Burton, S.A. & Babin, L.A. (1989) 'Decision making helps make the sale', *Journal of Consumer Marketing*, 6(Spring): 15–25.

Caballero, M.J., Lumpkin, J.R. & Madden, C.S. (1989) 'Using attractiveness as an advertising tool: an empircal test of the attraction phenomenon', *Journal of Advertising Research*, (Aug–Sept): 16–21.

Calder, A. (1969) *The People's War: Britain 1939–45*, London: Jonathan Cape.

Caldwell, J.T. (1954) *Televisuality: Style, Crisis and Authority in American Television*, New Jersey: Rutgers University Press.

Campbell, C. (1987) *The Romantic Ethic and the Spirit of Modern Consumerism*, Oxford: Macmillan.

Campbell, J. (1968) *Creative Mythology: the Masks of God*, New York: Viking Penguin.

Carroll, J.M.B. & Bever, T.G. (1976) 'Segmentation in cinema perception', *Science*, 191(March): 1053–4.

Castells, M. (1997) *The Power of Identity*, London: Blackwell.

Chisnall, P.M. (1985) *Marketing: a Behavioural Analysis*, London: McGraw-Hill.

Chisnall, P.M. (1992) *Marketing Research*, London, McGraw-Hill.

Cobb, R. (1995) 'The brains behind commercials: technology that reads viewers' grey matter as they watch prospective ads', *Marketing*.

Comfort, A. (1967) *The Anxiety Makers*, London: Thomas Nelson.

Coren, S. (1996) *Sleep Thieves: an Eye-Opening Exploration into the Science and Mysteries of Sleep*, New York: Free Press.

Coupey, E. A. & Jung. K. (1993) 'Influences of category structure on brand positioning and choice', University of Illinois, College of Commerce and Business Administration, Faculty Working Paper.

Csikszentmihalyi, M. & Rochberg-Halton, E. (1981) *The Meaning of Things: Domestic Symbols and the Self*, Cambridge: Cambridge University Press.

Cummings, C.H. (1999) 'Entertainment foods', *The Ecologist*, 29(1): 16–19.

Davidow, W.H. & Malone, M.S. (1992) *The Virtual Corporation: Structuring and Revitalizing the Corporation for the 21st Century*, New York: HarperCollins.

Davis, S. & Meyer, C. (1999) *Blur: the Speed of Change in the Connected Economy*, Oxford: Capstone.

Dawson, J.A. (1983) *Shopping Centre Development*, London: Longman.

De Chernatony, L. & MacDonald, M. (1992) *Creating Powerful Brands in Consumer, Service and Industrial Markets*, Oxford: Butterworth Heinemann.

Deighton J., Henderson, C.M. & Neslin S.A. (1994) 'The effects of advertising on brand switching and repeat purchasing', *Journal of Marketing Research*, 31(1, February): 28–44.

Dion, K.K. (1972) 'Physical attractiveness and evaluation of children's transgressions', *Journal of Personality and Social Psychology*, (24): 207–13.

Dion, K.K., Berscheid, E. & Walster, E. (1972) 'What is beautiful is good', *Journal of Personality and Social Psychology*, (24): 285–90.

Donnelly, J.H. (1996) *25 Management Lessons: from the Customer's Side of the Counter*, London: Irwin Professional Publishing.

Dowling, G.R.U. & Uncles, M. (1997) 'Do customer loyalty programs really work?', *Sloan Management Review*, Summer.

Drucker, P. (1992) *The Age of Discontent*, London: Transaction Publishing.

Drucker, P.F. (1994) *Post-Capitalist Society*, London: Butterworth-Heineman.

Dyson, P., Farr, A. & Hollis, N. (1996) 'Understanding, measuring, and using brand equity', *Journal of Advertising Research*, 36(6): 9–21.

Dyson, E. (1998) *Release 2.1*, London: Penguin.

Eales, J. (1998) 'Brand evaluation: horses for courses', *Market Leader*, 1(1): 43–7.

Edwards, P. (1998) 'The age of the trust brand', *Market Leader*, 3(1): 15–19.

Enis, B.M. & Cox, K.K. (1972) *Marketing Classics*, 6th edn, Boston, MA: Allyn and Bacon.

Etcoff, N. (1999) *Survival of the Prettiest: the Survival of Beauty*, London: Little, Brown.

FC&A (1997) *Top Secret Information the Government, Banks and Retailers Don't Want You to Know*, Peachtree City, GA: FC&A Publishing.

Falk, P. (1994) *The Consuming Body*, London: Sage.

Falk, P. & Campbell, C. (1997) *The Shopping Experience*, London: Sage.

Feather, F. (1997) *The Future Consumer*, New York: Warwick.

Feldman, E.B. (1967) *Varieties of Visual Experience*, New Jersey/New York, Prentice Hall/Harry N. Abrams.

Fleishman, E.A. (1967) *Studies in Personnel and Industrial Psychology*, Homewood, IL: Dorsey Press.

Fletcher, W. (1992) *A Glittering Haze: Strategic Advertising in the 1990s*, Henley-on-Thames: NTC Publications.

Foxall, G.R. (1977) *Consumer Behaviour: a Practical Guide*, Corbridge: Retail and Planning Associates.

Frank, R.H. (1999) *Why Money Fails to Satisfy in an Era of Success*, Cornell University/Free Press.

Frank, R.H. (1999) *Luxury Fever: Why Money Fails to Satisfy in an Era of Excess*, New York: Free Press.

Franzen, G. (1994) *Advertising Effectiveness*, Henley-on-Thames: NTC Publications.

Freidheim, C. (1998) *The Trillion-Dollar Enterprise: How the Alliance Revolution Will Transform Global Business*, New York: Perseus Books.

Freud, S. (1921) *Group Psychology and the Analysis of the Ego*, London: Hogarth.

Freud, S. (1930) *Civilisation and its Discontents*, London: Hogarth.

Fromm, E. (1942) *The Fear of Freedom*, London: Routledge and Kegan Paul.

Gabriel, Y. & Lang, T. (1995) *The Unmanageable Consumer: Contemporary Consumption and its Fragmentations*, London: Sage.

Galbraith, J.K. (1969) *The Affluent Society*, Harmondsworth: Penguin.

Gardner, B. (1963) *The Wasted Hour: the Tragedy of 1945*, London: Cassell.

Gardner, H. (1985) *The Mind's New Science: a History of the Cognitive Revolution*, New York: Basic Books.

Gershuny, J. (1988) 'Lifestyle, innovation and the future of work', *International Journal of Development Banking*, 6(1, January): 65–72.

Gibson, R. (1998) *Rethinking the Future*, London: Nicholas Brealey Publishing.

Gibson, W. (1995) *Neuromancer*, New York: Voyager.

Giddens, A. (1999) *Runaway World: How Globilization Is Restructuring Our Lives*, London: Profile Books.

Gilder, G. (1990) *Life After Television: the Coming Transformation of Media and American Life*, Knoxville, TN: Whittle Direct Books.

Gladwell, M. (1997) 'Annals of style – the coolhunt', *The New Yorker*, March 17th: 78–90.

Gleick, J. (1999) *Faster: the Acceleration of Just About Everything*, New York: Little, Brown.

Godin, S. (1999) *Permission Marketing: Turning Strangers into Friends, and Friends into Customers*, New York: Simon & Schuster.

Goffman, E. (1963) *Behaviour in Public Places*, New York: Free Press.

Goldberger, L. (ed.) (1982) *Handbook of Stress: Theoretical and Clinical Aspects*, New York: Free Press.

Grant, J. (1999) *The New Marketing Manifesto: the 12 Rules for Building Successful Brands in the 21st Century*, London: Orion.

Gross, R.D. (1992) *Psychology: the Science of Mind and Behaviour*, Cambridge: Hodder & Stoughton.

Gurvietz, P. (1997) 'Trust: a new approach to understanding the brand-consumer relationship, new and evolving paradigms', *Proceedings of the American Marketing Association Special Conference*, Dublin.

Guy, C.M. (1984) *Food and Grocery Shopping Behaviour in Cardiff*, Cardiff: Department of Town Planning, UWIST.

Haley, R.I. (1968) 'Benefit segmentation: a decision-oriented research tool', *Journal of Marketing*, 32: 30–35.

Hill, S. & Rifkin, G. (1999) *Radical Marketing: from Harvard to Harley, Lessons from Ten that Broke the Rules and Made It Big*, New York: HarperBusiness.

Hof, R.D. & Himelstein, L. (1999) 'eBay vs Amazon.com', *Business Week*, May 31st: 48–55.

Holland, P. (1997) *The Television Handbook*, London/New York: Routledge.

Hollinger, P. (1999) 'Stores develop ways to counter deep discounting', *Financial Times*.

Humphery, K. (1998) *Shelf Life: Supermarkets and the Changing Cultures of Consumption*, Cambridge: Cambridge University Press.

Hunt, M. (1993) *The Story of Psychology*, New York: Doubleday.

Institute of Personnel and Development. (1999) *Living to Work?* London: IPD.

Irons, K. (1998) 'Do you sincerely want to build relationships?', *Market Leader*, 3(1): 50–53.

Jacob, R. (1994) 'Why some customers are more equal than others,' *Fortune*, September 19th: 141–6.

Jauregi, J.A. (1995) *The Emotional Computer*, Oxford/Cambridge, MA: Blackwell.

Jeffreys, J.B. (1954) *Retail trading in Britain 1850–1950*, Cambridge: Cambridge University Press.

Jenkins, R. (1992) *Bringing Rio Home: Biodiversity in our Food and Farming*, London: Sustainable Agriculture, Food and Environment Alliance (SAFE).

Jensen, R. (1999) *The Dream Society*, New York: McGraw-Hill.

Jones, C. (1998) 'The next stage for brand equity in the US', *Market Leader*, 1(2): 64.

Kamp, E. M. & Macinnis, D.H. (1995) 'Characteristics of portrayed emotions in commercials: when does what is shown in ads affect viewers', *Journal of Advertising Research*, 35(6): 19–28.

Kaplan, B.M. (1985) 'Zapping – the real issue is communication', *Journal of Advertising Research*, 25(2): 9–12.

Kare-Silver, M.d. (1999) *e-shock: the Electronic Shopping Revolution: Strategies for Retailers and Manufacturers*, New York: American Management Association.

Kawasaki, G.M. (1999) *Rules for Revolutionaries*, London: HarperCollins.

Kelly, G.A. (1955) *The Psychology of Personal Constructs*, New York: W.W. Norton.

Kelly, K. (1995) *Out of Control*, London: Fourth Estate.

Kelly, K. (1998) *New Rules for the New Economy*, New York: Viking.

Keyfitz, N. (1992) 'Consumerism amd the new poor', *Society*, 29(2): 2–7.

Kortum, S. (1995) *The Hatless Man*, New York: Penguin.

Kotler, P. & Levy, S. (1969) 'Broadening the concept of marketing', *Journal of Marketing*, 33: 10–15.

Kotlowitz, A. et al. (1999) *Consuming Desires: Consumption, Culture, and the Pursuit of Happiness*, Washington: Island Press.

Kraft, R.N. (1986) 'The role of cutting in the evaluation and retention of film', *Journal of Experimental Psychology*, 12(1): 155–63.

Krishnan, H.S. & Chakravarti, D. (1999) 'Memory measurements for pretesting advertisements: an integrative conceptual framework and a diagnostic platform', *Journal of Consumer Psychology*, 8(1): 1–37.

LaBarbera, P.A. & Tucciarone, J.D. (1995) 'GSR reconsidered: a behavior-based approach to evaluating and improving the sales potency of advertising', *Journal of Advertising Research*, 35(5): 33–40.

Lancaster, G. (1992) 'Creating time for research', *Campaign* (August 6th).

Landfield, A.W. & Leitner, L.M. (1980) *Personal Construct Psychology*, New York: John Wiley.

Lane, R.E. (1991) *The Market Experience*, Cambridge: Cambridge University Press.

Lasch, C. (1984) *The Minimal Self: Psychic Survival in Troubled Times*, London: Pan Books.

Lasch, C. (1991) *The True and Only Heaven: Progress and its Critics*, New York: Norton.

Lebergott, S. (1993) *Pursuing Happiness: American Consumers in the Twentieth Century*, Princeton: Princeton University Press.

Lee, B. & Lee, R.S. (1995) 'How and why people watch TV: implications for the future of interactive television', *Journal of Advertising Research*, 35(6): 9–18.

Lee, M. (1993) *Consumer Culture Reborn: the Cultural Politics of Consumption*, London: Routledge.

Levine, R. (1997) *Geography of Time: the Temporal Misadventures of a Social Psychologist*, New York: Basic Books.

Levitt, T. (1960) 'Marketing myopia', *Harvard Business Review*, 35: 24–48.

Levy, S. (1982) 'Symbols, selves and others', *Advances in Consumer Research*, 9: 542–3.

Lewis, D. (1985) *Loving and Loathing: the Enigma of Personal Attraction*, London: Constable.

Lewis, D.D. (1989) *The Secret Language of Success: How to Read and Use Body-Talk*, London: Bantam Press.

Lewis, D.D. (1993) *Winning New Business*, London: Piatkus.

Lewis, D.D. (1996) *How To Get Your Message Across: a Practical Guide to Power Communication*, New York: Barnes and Noble.

Lewis, H.D. (1985) *Freedom and Alienation*, Edinburgh: Scottish Academic Press.

Lewis, P. (1975) *Just How Just?*, London: Secker and Warburg.

Lipsey, R.G. (1975) *An Introduction to Positive Economics*, London: Weidenfeld & Nicolson.

Longmate, N. (1973) *How We Lived Then: a History of Everyday Life during the Second World War*, London: Arrow Books.

Mack, J. & Lansley, S. (1985) *Poor Britain*, London: George Allen and Unwin.

Madge, J. (1963) *The Origins of Scientific Sociology*, London: Tavistock.

Markham, J.E. (1998) *The Future of Shopping: Traditional Patterns and Net Effects*, Basingstoke: Macmillan.

Martin, C. (1997) *The Digital Estate: Strategies for Competing, Surviving and Thriving in an Internetworked World*, New York: McGraw-Hill.

Martin, J. (1995) 'Ignore your customers', *Fortune*, May 1st: 82–6.

Martin, J.A. (1999) 'Spinning a new web: Publishers find creative ways to promote titles and authors – on the Internet', *Publishers Weekly*, April 26th: 36–9.

Maslow, A.H. (1968) *Towards a Psychology of Being*, 2nd edn, New Jersey: Van Nostrand.

Maslow, A.H. (1970) *Motivation and Personality*, 2nd edn, New York: Harper and Row.

McCracken, G. (1988) *Culture and Consumption: New Approaches to the Symbolic Character of Consumer Goods and Activities*, Bloomington: Indiana University Press.

Mcgovern G. (1999) *The Caring Economy: Business Principles for the New Digital Age*, Dublin: Blackhall Publishing.

Mick, D.G. (1986) 'Consumer research and semiotics: exploring the morphology of signs symbols and significance', *Journal of Consumer Research*, 13: 196–213.

Milgram, S. (1974) *Obedience to Authority*, London: Tavistock.

Miller, D. (1989) *A Theory of Shopping*, Cambridge: Polity Press.

Miller, D. (1995) *Acknowledging Consumption: a Review of New Studies*, London: Routledge.

Miller, D., Jackson, P., Thrift, N., Holbrook, B. & Rowlands, M. (1998) *Shopping, Place and Identity*, London/New York: Routledge.

Mitchell, V.W. & Bates, L. (1998) 'UK consumer decision making styles', *Journal of Marketing Management*, 14: 199–225.

Mitchell, V.W. & Boustani, P. (1992) 'Consumer risk perceptions in the breakfast cereal market', *British Food Journal*, 94(4): 17–27.

Negroponte, N. (1995) *Being Digital*, London, Hodder & Stoughton.

Neuborne, E. & Kerwin, K. (1999) 'Generation Y', *Business Week*: 44-50.

O'Brien, L. & Harris, F. (1991) *Retailing: Shopping, Society, Space*, London: David Fulton Publishers.

O'Dell, S.M. & Pajunen, J.A. (1997) *Butterfly Consumer*, Toronto: John Wiley.

Oliver, R.W. (1999) *The Shape of Things to Come*, London: McGraw-Hill.

O'Shaughnessy, J. (1987) *Why People Buy*, New York: Oxford University Press.

Ohanian, R. (1991) 'The impact of celebrity spokespersons on consumers' intention to purchase', *Journal of Advertising Research*, Feb–Mar: 46–52.

Osaka, M. (1979) 'Spectral analysis of EEG during mental activity', *Japanese Journal of Psychology*, 50(1): 45–8.

Packard, V. (1978) *The People Shapers*, Bucks: Futura.

Panofsky, E. (1993) *Meaning in the Visual Arts*, Harmondsworth: Penguin.

Pappenheim, F. (1959) *The Alienation of Modern Man*, New York/London: Modern Reader Paperbacks.

Park, C. W. & Young, M.S. (1986) 'Consumer response to television commercials: the impact of involvement and background music on brand attitude formation', *Journal of Marketing Research*, 23(1): 11–24.

Paulos, J.A. (1998) *Once upon a Number: the Hidden Mathematical Logic of Stories*, Harmondsworth: Penguin.

Paxton, A. (1994) *Food Miles*, London: Sustainable Agriculture, Food and Environment Allince (SAFE).

Pendergrast, M. (1993) *For God, Country and Coca-Cola*, London: Weidenfeld and Nicolson.

Pendergrast, M. (1999) *Uncommon Grounds: the History of Coffee and How it Transformed Our World*, New York: Basic Books.

Penn, R. (1971) 'Effects of motion and cutting rate in motion pictures', *AV Communication Review*, 19(1): 29–50.

Perrot, P. (1994) *Fashioning the Bourgeoisie: a History of Clothing in the Nineteenth Century*, New Jersey: Princeton University Press.

Perry, S.M. (1994) 'The Brand – Vehicle for Value in a Changing Marketplace', President's Lecture, London.

Peters, T.J. & Waterman, R.H. Jr. (1982) *In Search of Excellence*, New York: Harper & Row.

Pierce, J.R. & Noll, M. (1990) *Signals: the Science of Telecommunications*, New York: W.H. Freeman.

Pool, I.d.S. (1990) *Technologies Without Boundaries*, Cambridge, MA: Harvard University Press.

Pratkanis, A.R. & Aronson, E. (1992) *Age of Propaganda: the Everyday Use and Abuse of Persuasion*, New York/Oxford: W.H. Freeman.

Raven, H. (1995) *Off Our Trolleys? Food Retailing and The Hypermarket Economy*, London: Institute for Public Policy Research.

Reeves, B., Lang, A., Thorson, E. & Rothschild, M. (1989) 'Emotional television scenes and hemispheric specialisation', *Human Communication Research*, 15(4): 493–508.

Reichheld, F.F. (1996) *The Loyalty Effect*, Boston, MA: Harvard Business School Press.

Rheingold, H. (1994) *The Virtual Community: Finding Connection in a Computerized World*, London: Martin Secker & Warburg.

Ries, A. (1996) *Focus: the Future of Your Company Depends on it*, London: HarperCollins.

Roof, W. C. (1999) *Spiritual Marketplace*, Princeton, NJ: Princeton University Press.

Rosen, E. (2000) *The Anatomy of Buzz: How to Create Word-of-Mouth Marketing*, New York: Currency Doubleday.

Rosenberg, L. (1998) *Breath by Breath*, London: HarperCollins.

Rosenblatt, R. (ed.) (1999) *Consuming Desires: Consumption, Culture and the Pursuit of Happiness*, Washington, D.C.: Shearwater Books.

Roskies, E. (1987) *Stress Management for the Healthy Type A*, New York: The Guilford Press.

Rothschild, M.L., Thorson, E., Reves, B., Hirsch, J.E. & Goldstein, R. (1986) 'EEG activity and the processing of television commercials', *Communication Research*, 13(2): 182–220.

Rothschild, M.L., Hyun, Y.J., Reeves, B., Thorson, E. & Goldstein, R. (1988) 'Hemispherically lateralized EEG as a response to television commercials', *Journal of Consumer Research*, 15(September): 185–94.

Rothschild, M.L., Hyun, Y.J., Reeves, B., Thorson, E. & Goldstein, R. (1990) 'Predicting memory for components of TV commercials from EEG', *Journal of Consumer Research*, 16(March): 472–8.

Rucci, A.J., Kirn, S.P. & Quinn, R.T. (1998) 'The employee–customer profit chain at Sears', Harvard Business Review (Jan–Feb): 83–97.

Salt, B. (1977) 'Film style and technology in the forties', *Film Quarterly*, 31: 46–57.

Sampson, P. (1993) 'A better way to brand image', *Admap*, 28(7 July/August): 19–24.

Samuelson, P. & Nordhaus, W.S. (1989) *Economics*, New York: McGraw-Hill.

Schelling, T.C. (1978) *Micromotives and Macrobehaviour*, New York/London: W.W. Norton.

Schneider, B. & Bowen, D.E. (1995) *Winning the Service Game*, Boston, MA: Harvard Business School Press.

Searle, J.R. (1995) *The Construction of Social Reality*, Harmondsworth: Penguin.

Seybold, B.P. (1998) *Customers.com: How to Create a Profitable Business Strategy for the Internet*, London: Random House.

Shapiro, C. and Varian, H.R. (1999) *Information Rules: a Strategic Guide to the Network Economy*, Boston, MA: Harvard Business School Press.

Sherrington, M. (1998) 'Market segmentation really is cool', *Market Leader*, 1(1): 22–5.

Silverstein, S. (1974) *Where the Sidewalk Ends*, New York: HarperCollins.

Simmons, J. (1964) *The Changing Pattern of Retail Location*, University of Chicago, Department of Geography.

Skinner, B.F. (1972) *Beyond Freedom and Dignity*, New York: Bantam Books/Vintage Books.

Solomon, M.R. (1999) *Consumer Behaviour*, New Jersey: Prentice-Hall.

Stern, B.L. & Resnik, A.J. (1991) 'Information content in television advertising: a replication and extension', *Journal of Advertising Research*, (June–July): 36–46.

Stone, G.P. (1954) 'City shoppers and urban identification', *American Journal of Sociology*, 60: 36–45.

Stouffer, S.A., Guttman, L., Lazarsfeld, P.F. and Star, S.A. (1949–1950) *Studies in Social Psychology in World War II*, Princeton, NJ: Princeton University Press.

Stout, A. & Burda, B.L. (1989) 'Zipped commercials: are they effective?', *Journal of Advertising*, 18(4): 23–32.

Sudman, S. & Schwarz, N. (1989) 'Contributions of cognitive psychology to advertising research', *Journal of Advertising Research*, June–July: 43–53.

Sutherland, M. (1993) *Advertising and the Mind of the Consumer*, St Leonards: Allen & Unwin.

Swinyards, W.R. (1998) 'Shopping mall customer values: the national mall shopper and the list of values', *Journal of Retailing and Consumer Services*, 5(3): 167–72.

Symon, C. (1998) 'E-business: the inevitable future', *Market Leader*, 1(1): 48–51.

Tajfel, H. (1981) *Human Groups and Social Categories*, Cambridge: Cambridge University Press.

Thomson, K. (1998) 'Profitable relationships come from inside out', *Market Leader*, 1(2): 58–61.

Tomkins, R. (1999) 'Fading stars of the global stage', *Financial Times*: 10.

Townsend, P. (1993) *The International Analysis of Poverty*, Hemel Hempstead: Harvester Wheatsheaf.

Twitchell, J.B. (1999) *Lead Us into Temptation: the Triumph of American Materialism*, Columbia University Press.

Tyrrell, B. & Westall, T. (1998) 'The new service ethos, a post-brand future – and how to avoid it', *Market Leader*, 1(2): 14–19.

Underhill, P. (1999) *Why We Buy: the Science of Shopping*, London: Orion.

Vandermerwe, S. (1999) *Customer Capitalism*, London: Nicholas Brealey Publishing.

Vanhonacker, W.R. (1993) 'What does the multinomial logic model really measure?, INSEAD, Research and the Development of Pedagogical Materials Working Paper.

Wallace, P. (1999) *Agequake: Riding the Demographic Rollercoaster, Shaking Business, Finance and our World*, London: Nicholas Brealey Publishing.

Walton, P. & Gamble, A. (1972) *From Attention to Surplus Value*, London: Sheed and Ward.

Watson, J.B. (1913) 'Psychology as the behaviourist views it', *Psychology Review*, (20): 158–77.

Weizenbaum, J. (1976) *Computer Power and Human Reason: From Judgement to Calculation*, Harmondsworth: Penguin.

Williamson, J. (1978) *Decoding Advertisements*, New York: Marion Boyars.

Willis, P. (1990) *Common Culture: Symbolic Work at Play in the Everyday Cultures of the Young*, Milton Keynes: Open University Press.

Wilson, C. (1956) *The Outsider: the Classic Study of Alienation, Creativity and the Modern Mind*, London: Indigo.

Wilson, J. (1993) 'Mindfood – developing brands for a harder-thinking new generation of consumers', *Admap*, February (326): 17–19.

Wolf, M.J. (1999) *The Entertainment Economy*, New York: Times Books.

Wolfe, J.M. (1997). 'In a blink of the mind's eye', Nature, 387(19 June): 756–7.

Wurman, R.S. (1991) *Information Anxiety*, London: Pan Books.

Young, H. (1990) *One of Us*, London, Pan Books.

Young, P. (1991) *Person to Person: the International Impact of the Telephone*, Cambridge, Granta.

Zakharova, N. N. & Avdeyev, V.N. (1982) 'Functional changes in the CNS during perception of music: on the problem of studying positive emotions', *Zhurnal Vysshei Nervnoi Deyatel'nostic*, 32(5): 915–24.

Zepp, I.G. (1997) *The New Religious Image of Urban America: the Shopping Mall as Ceremonial Center*, Colorado: University Press of Colorado.

Index